One in Christ

by K. E. Skydsgaard

Translated by Axel C. Kildegaard

MUHLENBERG PRESS · PHILADELPHIA

PREFACE

Except for the first chapter, this small book contains in somewhat revised form a series of lectures concerning Roman Catholicism and Protestantism which were given during the spring semester, 1953, at the People's University in Copenhagen. Therein lie the scope and the limitations of the book. It does not pretend to be an exhaustive treatment of this broad and burning problem.

I consider this book an experiment and a quest, and ask that Roman Catholic as well as Evangelical readers approach it in the same manner. It is not written to widen divisions or to make differences greater, but to contribute to mutual understanding. The purpose is not polemic, but is to serve as an introduction to questions that have become of vital significance for the Christian church, and with which many people today are concerned. There are many large and learned works that also deal with the subject of this book. It is necessary to work with these if one would really attempt to grasp the situation fully.

There is also a great deal of popular literature on this subject. Most of what I have read of the latter, both from the Roman and the Evangelical camps, has not appealed to me. As a rule it is too much like propaganda, too cheap, and too greatly simplified. Roman Catholics and Protestants have each in their own way been tempted to dismiss each other with certain established battle clichés that in the course of time have acquired an almost magical power over the minds of men. It is difficult to escape that danger, but we must do all we can to remain free from it. It poisons the relationship between the two groups and is unworthy in a spiritual contest. Those who wish to have the entire question clarified by some obviously plain and manageable points of view which free them from the need to take a stand themselves will, I hope, be disappointed with this book. But it is my hope that the book will prove helpful to those who wish to work with the question in a more basic way.

The book is written from a particular point of view, and out of an Evangelical Lutheran conviction, but that does not mean that everything is clarified. My own opinions and views are still open to further study and illumination. This has at times given me a painful feeling of incompleteness, but it has also been a joy to grapple anew with a great and significant question. If it should happen that a Roman Christian should understand a little more of Evangelical Christianity by reading this small volume, and that an Evangelical Christian should have a little better grasp of what is central in the Roman Catholic church, and that they both, through this experience, see something of the "yes" which binds them together and the "no" which separates them, the author will be grateful.

K. E. Skydsgaard

CONTENTS

Chapter 1

FELLOWSHIP AND DIVISION

The so-called ecumenical movement is an essential feature in the life and history of the Christian church today. What meaning is to be found in this movement? Is the concern for unity and fellowship between Christians throughout the world and among various Christian church organizations something unimportant, perhaps even mistaken? Is this a superficial movement that will soon disappear as have many other such movements, without leaving a trace? The answer to these questions depends on what one understands the ecumenical movement to be.

If the ecumenical movement concerns that which is basically essential in Christianity only in an incidental and superficial manner, it will soon disappear, and there will be no cause to grieve over it. If, on the other hand, the movement expresses something in Christianity which unmistakably belongs to it, it has a right to live, and its development should not be hindered.

Nothing on this earth is so sublime and true that it cannot be perverted and misunderstood—perhaps even distorted into a caricature of itself. It almost seems as if the more vital a matter is, the more destined it is to be misunderstood and the more disastrous it is when this happens. All efforts must be dedicated to cleanse the ecumenical

1

movement from all that is incidental and irrelevant. Then it becomes a call we cannot ignore.

It is essential first to establish the truth that there is a fervent and completely intimate relationship between the genuine and central strength of the ecumenical movement and Christianity itself, and that the ecumenical impulse belongs to and springs forth from the very nature of Christianity.

Christianity is fellowship—not only in the sense that it must always and obviously always has had consequences in the social sphere, but because Christianity in its innermost nature, in its supernatural mystery, *is* fellowship. Fellowship is not just something that "happens," but is bound up with God's own nature and God's will toward his humanity. In our belief that God is love, we are asserting that God is the God of fellowship, for it is the nature of love to give and to create community.

We find in saying that Christianity is fellowship: 1) the mystery of creation, for God created out of love by communicating life and making men the sharers of life with him and mutually with one another; 2) sin's insoluble enigma, for the nature of sin is to break fellowship with God and fellow man in unbelief, selfishness, and isolation; and 3) the miracle of salvation, for of this does God's saving work consist: that God in Christ re-establishes the broken fellowship, both between himself and man and between men mutually. Everything in Christ—his incarnation and his life as well as his death and his resurrection—springs forth from and aims toward the fellowship of love.

As God raises up fallen humanity to fellowship with himself, he also unites men with one another. Christianity can never exist as the possession of a single individual, but is always the possession of a fellowship, that is to say, a church. This is the very thing to which the church testifies—that God has not created so many individual relationships between himself and mankind, but that God has created a fellowship in which a man does not exist for his own sake either in relationship to God or to his fellows. God created men to live in fellowship. Isolation, dissension, and self-sufficiency are exactly contrary to man's true purpose here on earth. That God saves always means that man is saved from his loneliness and self-centeredness and enters into a new community with God and mankind. God's new creation is humanity which is redirected homeward toward its destiny—to live in fellowship with God and with one another. According to his decision, the church is the beginning of the renewal of the entire creation.

The strongest expression for this fellowship is found in the New Testament words which describe the church as the "body of Christ," expressing that intimate relationship both between Christ and the congregation and between the members of the body themselves. "That they may all be one; even as thou, Father, art in me, and I in thee, that they also may be in us . . ." (John 17:21). Fellowship between men in the church of Christ has as its model, and has also the same nature as, that fellowship which exists between the Son and the Father in the oneness of love. Fellowship has its source in the very heart of God.

The degree to which the idea of fellowship is underlined in recent studies of the New Testament and of the earliest Christian church, is remarkable. The New Testament, as well as the early church, is permeated with the view of the congregation as a unity, in which the individual does not exist in and of himself, but only has life in fellowship with the others. Christianity is a fellowship which extends itself out toward all mankind on earth. It is a communion, *koinonia*, where the principal sin is to isolate oneself, to cut oneself off from others in pride and self-sufficiency. "Preserve me, Lord, from that grievous sin which I fear so greatly: from hatred toward your love; so that I may not sin against that Holy Spirit which is love, unity, peace, and harmony," said one of the early church fathers.

Christian fellowship is equally far removed from an individualism where the unique is worshiped for its own sake, whether under secular or pious signs. It is also far from a so-called fellowship which is more or less forced upon people, and where the individual is drowned, without responsibility and without personality, in an anonymous crowd. This is true whether the collection of individuals has a more secular or a more pious name: community, state, or church. The fellowship of Christians is always giving and receiving, and free relationship between persons.

The church in its innermost nature is a fellowship, not in outer, external uniformity, but in a unity of faith, hope, and love. It is called to be the true fellowship in the midst of a world which tears itself to pieces in discord and strife, where either the individual or individuals pervert the great word of freedom into a privilege for themselves and their own egotistical interests, or where the community is misused to crush and strangle the individual. "O Milieu, that takes away our persons," says Lars Ahlin in his novel, *Fromma Mord* (*Pious Murder*). And we could add to that: "O holy individualism, that takes away our neighbor."

The church was called to witness to that true fellowship to which God in Christ redeemed his created humanity.

"O Lamb of God that takest away the sin of the world," is the refrain that sounds in the Christian congregation. To take away sins means precisely to take away that which kills fellowship. Where there is forgiveness of sin, there is life and holiness, because a way is thereby opened upward toward God and outward toward fellow man. In fellowship with Christ and with our neighbor, heaven is already here on earth.

The apostolic congregation echoes the great message that in Christ all are one. "There is neither Jew nor Greek, there is neither slave nor free, there is neither male nor female; for you are all one in Christ Jesus" (Gal. 3:28). God's plan of salvation was "a plan for the fulness of time, to unite all things in him, things in heaven and things on earth" (Eph. 1:10). "Rather, speaking the truth in love, we are to grow up in every way into him who is the head, into Christ, from whom the whole body, joined and knit together by every joint with which it is supplied, when each part is working properly, makes bodily growth and up-builds itself in love" (Eph. 4:15-16). Just as there is but one Christ, one cross, and one resurrection, so there is only one fellowship, one body, one baptism, and one eucharist where they all can meet. So also there is only one Holy Spirit, which creates unity and fellowship. Therefore there cannot be many separated churches or denominations each with its own confession, each with its own Lord's Table.

In this way, we have already said that the church of Christ exists today in a situation which is not in agreement with its purpose. That which according to the will of Christ was an impossibility is actually today a reality in our midst. The "impossible" has become a reality! In this is to be found the church's paradoxical condition.

It is a recognition of this which lies behind the ecumenical movement among all the churches today. There is something here that never again will cease to cause grief and pain, no matter how many explanations we manage to present. The division of the church is not something which we shall try to explain and thereby remove from the world —for that which one can explain has in the final analysis lost its impact. It is a burden which we shall try to carry together and which, in a certain, manner, already ties and unites the churches to one another.

In the following we shall consider two of the contending parties—the Roman Catholic and the Evangelical Lutheran churches. As a beginning, let us pose the following question: How shall the Christian churches conduct themselves when disagreements arise concerning what Christianity is? In the final analysis it is on this question that the cleavage between the churches arises. Naturally, many social, sociological, and psychological factors are involved—perhaps more than we realize. These are all the divisive matters which we in our day include under the designation, "non-theological factors." Nevertheless, it is not these which are determinative. The controversy and consequent division which is serious and determinative rises from the apparent or perhaps completely real difference in belief, teaching, and understanding of the central aim and goal of the gospel.

In the face of such penetrating differences there are two completely different basic points of view that largely govern current ways of thinking. We can designate these points of view with the catchwords: "subjectivism" and "objectivisim."

"Subjectivism" maintains that the more opinions that

exist the better. Religious truth must always remain something individual. The individual must on his own responsibility arrive at his own conceptions and give expression to his own belief. Religious truth is so rich and many-sided that it cannot be exhausted by a single system, but is mirrored only by many interpretations. There is actually no ground for strife, for although the ways may be different, the goal remains the same. For this reason the main theme of subjectivism is one of toleration and spaciousness with equal place for the most extreme points of view. They are in the last analysis equally true, and even if they should not be that, the individual would still have his unrestricted right in freedom to believe about Christianity whatever he wished. The various developments are expressions of religious experience that cannot be adequately contained in any one system of human thought.

"Objectivism" grasps the matter completely otherwise. There is only one truth which God has revealed and before which men must submit. It is possible to formulate this truth in a clear and intellectually comprehensible manner which must be uniform and binding upon all. The Christian church has one wholly definite teaching. It has completely defined dogmas. Here on principle there can be no talk of toleration but only of authority, a final court which tells the individual what it is that he shall believe and do. It can be the pope's infallible doctrinal authority, it can be orthodoxy's interpreted Bible, it can be the individual church's tradition through the ages. It can also be the most unorthodox understanding of Christianity. The matter becomes somewhat the same.

It is self-evident that subjectivism has had its stronghold within the tradition of modern Protestantism while ob-

jectivism most consistently is represented by Catholicism.
But for that matter the lines of division are found not only
between the various denominations but most often cut
right through these.

According to the view of subjectivism, unity is maintained by one man or one group, with certain particular
opinions, understanding that the opinions of the other man
or group in and of themselves can be just as good as their
own, and in any case that the other man or group has unrestricted right to have these opinions. The difference lies
partly in the different individual characters and their
various psychological presuppositions. The only thing I
have a right to demand is that the other give to me the
same right that I give to him. According to this conception,
the church becomes the community of all these people with
their diverse conceptions and forms of expressions, the
spacious framework about these different men and their
individual, freely formed conceptions of faith.

For objectivism the issues resolve themselves differently.
Unity here is derived from the fact that religious authority
is respected and followed. The individual submits himself
in freedom, or, if necessary, although it may be against his
inclination and desire, to the common authority. All things
considered, there can be no talk here of spaciousness or
toleration. The church is the community of men who are
united in faith and doctrinal confession. Its priests cannot
be individually free but are duty bound by the teachings of
the church. If the individual cannot submit himself to the
religious authority, whatever form this may take, he must
go his own way. If he refuses to do this, by one way or
another means must be found to force him out.

The principle of authority is most consistently carried

out in the Roman Catholic church but in most churches the same is more or less true: there is a religious, Christian authority which is binding upon the individual, naturally upon the ministers in particular.

We have now distinguished between two apparently opposite points of view and we have intentionally drawn the contrast with very bold and strong strokes. Our purpose now is not to enter more deeply into the question, or to try to improve the picture by adding the subtle shadings, to judge between the points of view. On the contrary, we will pose a question: Is it only by one of these two methods—subjectivism or objectivism—that true unity can be established between Christians? Is there no other way? Are we forced from the start to choose one of these two possibilities? Many will maintain (and their stand will be quite secure as far as pure logic goes) that here there is a clear "either-or." Either one is a subjectivist or one is an objectivist, as I have above attempted to define these points of view. Are they right? Or could there be another way to consider—a way that is perhaps more difficult, less surveyed and charted, but truer and more consistent with Christianity itself in its own inner life and mystery? Is it not as if these two ways—subjectivism and objectivism— are in conspiracy with two other ways by which men today are seeking to escape from chaos—individualism and collectivism? But neither individualism nor collectivism is capable of creating true fellowship. Each attempts to do so in its own way, but these attempts misfire before our eyes. The same may be said of the ways of subjectivism and objectivism.

We will try to sketch another way. This may prove difficult but the implications may be valuable.

What is actually the innermost essence of Christianity? Is it one or another religious philosophy or metaphysic, a collection of lofty Christian doctrines, one or another ethic or moral, one or another way of life or understanding of existence? None of these. This does not mean that these things do not in one way or another have their place in Christendom. For, of course, Christianity also has to do with understanding life, with ethics and ways of life, with doctrines, and with philosophy as well, but it will never be proper to say that any of these is the essential. If one would for example try to define Christianity in terms of any one of these things, and perhaps even "proof text" this to excess with Bible passages, one would completely miss the mark. As true as it may be, as penetrating and lofty, as "lifelike" and for the modern man as "understandable," whether under the banner of subjectivism or objectivism, nevertheless there would still be lacking that one thing which is the essential and unique feature of Christianity.

It was not with any of these that the Apostles went forth and with which they "conquered the world." The essential in all that they said and did and by which they lived was not a "something" but a real, living *person*, Jesus Christ himself. The innermost and intrinsic reality, without which all else would be empty form, was the belief in and the worshipful confession of Jesus Christ as the living Lord. A living Lord must be something more than a view of life, or ethic, or dogmatic, or understanding of existence. All these are but implements or forms of expression for the basic relationship, the relationship to a living person. Before one line of the New Testament was written, before a single proof text came into being, there was a church which lived in faith upon and obedience toward a living

Lord, Jesus himself. For this reason the resurrection plays such a determinative role in the witness of the New Testament, from which all else receives its new and unique illumination. Everything which we can call ethic and understanding of life in the New Testament receives its content and its life out of this faith in the Risen One.

There has not been one moment in the life of the church when it has not in one way or another confessed this living, crucified, resurrected, risen, and ascended Lord. He was made the foundation of all, both of life here on earth and the hope of the resurrection and fulfilment in eternity. This did not depend upon any proof text, but only upon the risen Lord himself. The New Testament gives us a manifold and variegated and by no means a uniform expression of this faith. Any attempt to make one or another dogmatic or ethical lawbook out of this will run up against great difficulties. But behind it all, as the red thread that ties everything together, is the living Christ himself. The truth was a person. And that will always be something far more than a book, even with the loftiest rules of life or the most existential understanding of self. The early church did not try to express this in a philosophy or in a particularly supernatural metaphysic. It spoke of these things in completely personal terms, in words of action. Without in any way pretending to make this "philosophically" understandable, they witnessed to a reality that was beyond understanding and without comparison in the history of man.

If this viewpoint is securely held—and I believe that here we are in the unique world of the New Testament, the world of the early church—we will be able to understand that this matter of being unified first and last must consist of being in fellowship with this Lord, of hearing his Word,

of joining together in the common singing of praise and
worship, and of entering into this obedience toward him
alone. However great significance teaching and doctrine
can and as a matter of fact do have, here we are on entirely
different ground.

Of course there must be definite doctrines, for Christ
was not a misty figure who could be interpreted in many
different ways. The risen Lord was identical with that
Jesus with whom his followers had wandered together on
the country roads of Galilee, whom they had seen with tax
collectors and sinners, the poor and the obscure, the sick
and the lame. Now they witnessed to others about what
they had seen. And this witness received definite outer
expressions and forms. This is right and important, but it
must never be forgotten that to tear all this away from the
living Lord who rules freely and supremely in his church,
will make Christianity into some form of "orthodoxy" of
religious knowledge and information that completely
misses the point. A "dogma" about the Christ is not the
same as a witness to the living Lord. Christ himself is
always more than even the richest doctrine about his
person.

It was not at all peculiar that different conceptions
should arise in the church. These different conceptions
could in no way disturb the unity if only one would hold
securely to the witness to the living Lord. Wouldn't it have
been a sign of great poverty and tedium if there could
have been but one conception, one opinion, one viewpoint? At a matter of fact, the early congregation was not
so spiritless. A Jew in Palestine could not conceive of the
Christ in the same manner as a Greek Christian in Corinth.
There was a difference between Paul and John and James

and Peter and their congregations; yes, there is a difference between Matthew, Mark, and Luke. Had the whole matter hinged upon a teaching, or a religious philosophy, or an understanding of life, then there might have been a completely different kind of unity and uniformity. But this was not so, because it was above all the living Lord who stood at the center. Where the Lord and the spirit of the Lord are, there is freedom, Paul says—a freedom which at the same time is a bond to the one Lord.

Behind all these differences there lies an unusual unity which, if most profoundly seen, consists of this: behind and transcending all the ways of expression there was something infinitely greater than the expressions themselves, namely the living person of Christ. For this reason Paul did not say to John, "Your way of expressing this matter is wrong; mine alone is right." There could certainly have arisen tensions, and strife, but as long as fellowship around the living Lord existed, unity was not broken. Also down through the ages there has been tension and strife. In and of itself there is nothing evil in this. Wouldn't it have been unthinkable if there had not been this in a congregation on earth?

The Christian witness is not dead witness. The Christian church consists of living men gathered in obedience toward a risen Lord, and naturally there will arise contradictions and disturbances in the relationships between all these peoples of all sorts of cultures and races with the most varied psychological conditionings and temperaments, with the most varied life conditions and questions of life. Should there not also rise then a living movement in the understanding of how Christianity can express itself, of how one becomes a Christian, even of whom Christ is?

Grundtvig distinguished between the church and the school. That is, in the church we are all one; there discussion is silenced and we are united to hear, to praise and to confess, to receive, to cut through the various interpretations. We are united in the same confession, even though we may not understand its particular parts in the same manner. And we are together with peoples of other races and colors, people whose ways of thinking we do not know on the whole; yet we do know that we are a unit or perhaps more correctly, one, for the Lord is the same, Savior, Son of God, our brother. But in the "school," opinions may have free scope. Here the problems must be worked and discussed, and here there shall surely also be strife and combat. And naturally this risk contains the possibility that a real disagreement and split may break out, as there is risk in all that lives. But in itself, it is only natural that there are different conceptions which are all held together by Christ himself, who is greater than our interpretation of him.

As an example, there were in the worship life of Denmark the Inner Mission Movement and Grundtvigianism—two schools that were widely different and which could battle with one another but which nevertheless were one in the church. At a meeting held some time ago where the discussion raged strongly and where theological opinions were widely separated, one of the participants in the discussion made this remark in his final plea: "The preceding speaker and I are in the same church and there we are one, for we confess the same Lord and Savior, but in the school we are in complete disagreement, and there we must dispute." There was a unity more profound than the evident differences. The divergent opinions did not destroy it.

But we must go another step. What I have said will surely gain the assent of many. But the problem of the church today does not lie in the different viewpoints in the "school," while unanimous and common praise and confession is heard in the church. The pain lies in this very matter of the "impossible"—disunity has broken out in the church itself.

What shall we do about a situation which is impossible according to the intent of Christ, yet has actually happened? That which is the nature of sin—to divide and split, to destroy and cripple fellowship—has invaded the church itself, not only as a constant temptation and weakness but as a situation that is accepted, and almost declared to be normal. And this happens not only on the larger scale, but even in the single, local congregation.

One thing must be said first of all: Christ is the living Lord also over the division. This is not a casual and simply pious way of speaking, but a completely necessary conclusion from that gospel of Christ which comes to us out of the New Testament. Christ is Lord—also over that church which has been invaded by division and strife. He does his work throughout this church; even its division he will and does use in his service. Just as sinful disunity is a mystery (*mysterium iniquitatis*), so the power of Christ in a divided church is a mystery, a mystery of grace and mercy.

Before there can be any talk of unity, of the ecumenical movement, or of the community between the churches, there stands the confession of Christ as the Lord. And this will—strange as it may sound—give witness to the fact that in him we are already one church, we are already one. For the divided church is also under his atonement and under the power of his resurrection. In his good time, Christ will realize that unity which no human power (nor that of a church which allows the powers of division to penetrate into itself) can do anything about. Without this premise, which truly enough can only be maintained in faith, every effort for the unity of the church is doomed in advance to be a futile labor of building a tower of Babel. We may go the way of subjectivism or the way of objectivism; both will lead us away from our goal, for both basically fail to appreciate that secret which is to be found in faith in the living Lord. In the last analysis, both travel in one manner or another the way of human logic, and thus they are perhaps not so different as they appeared to be at first.

Our efforts toward unity inevitably become forced whenever unity is seen as something we have to work out. In our common confession of Christ as Lord, we are released from this compulsion. In the same moment a mighty truth is heard: In Christ you are already one. In Christ the "churches" are also united into one body. Out of this alone comes the command: Become that which you are. Work on that which already is a reality in Christ.

The church is always on a pilgrimage. On this pilgrimage strange powers have invaded the church—including the evil spirit of division which is sin against the spirit of love, unity, peace, and harmony. The same spirit which tempts mankind to fall away from community with God and fellow man and which cripples God's whole creation, assaults God's church and to all appearances has triumphed. But Christ is nevertheless Lord. Without faith in this, all work for unity and fellowship is a drudgery under the law which either leads to the self-righteousness of the Pharisees or to despair. In faith which rests upon Christ as Lord, we are freed from both alternatives, freed to work for unity and fellowship in the joy of the gospel.

It is in this faith that we now seriously ask: What shall we do, we who today live as divided churches, who perhaps even experience that division within the same denomination and church? The question does not become less serious and pressing under the all-embracing premise which we have just discussed. Just the opposite! But now there is a possibility that it may be posed rightly and in truth. This will mean, among other things, that it is posed in repentance and in hope. And it means that those ways which so naturally offered themselves to us—subjectivism or objectivism—show themselves to be completely inadequate, so amazingly shortsighted and, in relationship to the concern which now occupies us, both contrived and earthbound. We succumb all too easily to these ideas and must constantly be freed from their binding power.

The real disagreement in the church can cause an exceedingly critical situation in which the only possibility is to say a plain and clear "no." That church which cannot say "no," can probably not say "yes." At any rate there is no power in its "yes." As someone once put it: That church which cannot curse cannot bless.

Between the Roman Catholic and the Evangelical Lutheran churches there was once expressed a mighty "no." It sounded from both sides and it sounded in such a way that it was heard. And it has sounded again and again in one way or another down to the present day. It has not been said lightly for there has been awareness on both sides of what it meant. A real breach came in unity for it was not only a verbal battle in the "school." It led to a division in the church. And this is a frightful thing.

But this "no" could not have been genuine had there not also been together with it a "yes" between the two parties. Both the "yes" and the "no" must work and become articulate. Subjectivism concerns itself with both of these only superficially for it is an expression of an irenic attitude which in the last analysis has no passion for the truth but considers the problem between the two parties as solved for all time. Objectivism also considers the question closed, although in another manner. It knows no other way than victory or defeat for one or the other party.

But both are false solutions. The church which believes in the living Lord will endure the division without ever accepting it. It will remain upon the way, and there it will live with both the burden of the "no" and the promise and hope of the "yes" until the hour of unity appears. The principal concern for Roman Catholics and Evangelical Lutherans today, strange as it may sound, is not that they are divided, but how they can live with one another in the division, how they can say their "yes" and say their "no." They are in a strange manner obligated in both respects. They are not called upon to isolate themselves from each other but to walk with one another on the way with their mutual "yes" and "no." What matters to God is the manner in which they now, in a situation of division, walk and talk with each other.

But situations can also arise within the same church where a "no" must be expressed. The Scandinavian Lutheran churches must, as a consequence of their development, have room for different concepts. They can never become cliques of Christian uniformity and unanimity. But they can provide a ground for tensions which can, on occasion, be extremely difficult to bear. There can also come that moment when a "no" must be heard. A church that tries to obey Christ can find itself in a situation where the only honest solution is the "no" and the separation. Such a "no" presupposes a responsible action under a risk; it demands both awareness and courage, and, for that matter, a purity which is free from the perhaps unconscious temptation to persecute others.

This does not mean that every "no" is genuine and that it is right to follow every cry of "no" and exclusion and all that implies. On the contrary, it can very well be through shortsightedness a false negation which the church is called upon to make. Not every negation is either pure or genuine. In the course of time the church's "no" has often been extremely tarnished. Both between denominations and within individual churches a very impure "no" has been said. And it has also been hasty and rash.

The "no" is the last possibility, and it is not always the right one. Disagreements can arise in the church which the church must by all means try to fight its way through. In a disagreement which threatens to break the fellowship, the determining factor is not that the disagreement arises, but how it is solved and how the disagreeing parties speak and work with one another. A dispute puts the parties concerned on trial. At present I am convinced that the living Lord is more interested in how his church conducts the dispute that has arisen than in the causes of the controversy. A dispute or a battle in the church can expose that which is the most tragic within men—both the extremely doubtful joy of setting oneself up against the traditional by the often cheap triumph over one's perhaps mediocre opponents, and the anxious indignation of the orthodox that there might be found the slightest crack in the iron kettle of orthodoxy.

Much is demanded of us in situations of dispute, both when our relationships to other denominations and to those with whom we are in disagreement in our own church are concerned. Just as courage may be called for in order to say "no," there is also courage in the willingness truly to go into that which the opponent maintains, to "stand outside of ourselves" in order to try to find that truth which might lie in the opponent's view which we ourselves may have overlooked. There is always courage necessary to concede that I have thought and considered wrongly, at any rate shortsightedly and insufficiently. The one who talks big and to all appearances is the strongest and most convinced, is not always the one who acts most carefully and with the most courage. Nor is it always those who establish the right that are right. Far from it.

We are on the way together and the gospel's word about cautiousness and soberness in the one who walks with his opponent on the way is relevant also for those who have fallen into dispute, even division. This word of the gospel is relevant to a church and it is relevant to the churches. This word can be decisive if we are clear on the fact that the final authority in the church is not ourselves, whoever we may be, but the living Lord himself.

It could be that the living Lord has his very specific questions to pose which would not be so simple to answer and which could not be answered on the premises of either subjectivism or objectivism. Both subjectivism and objectivism see and answer the question "from below," from our side, but in the church the question sounds to us from the living Lord himself. He will have questions that he will pose to both parties, both to the "traditional" and to the "revolutionary." "You say that those here, or those there, deny me and estrange themselves from the truth. You maintain that you are doing a good work by hurling out your 'no' and doing all within your means to stop the others. Are you certain that it is a good work toward me? You with your cut-and-dried confessions, with all the right words, with the correct piety, and the right doctrines, with which you now even decide what is right and correct.

"And you rebels who are breaking tradition—are you so certain of the way which you are traveling? You stand and speak so with such prophetic cocksureness, but does it amount to much? You triumph over others, you enjoy your free spirit, your discovery. You forge ahead, but who are you? Is it for *my* sake that you forge ahead, or could there be other motives?"

In a church that bears the name of Christ we are never alone and therefore never free from the living One himself, whether we are of the one or the other party

Disagreement and strife on the way demand much more of us than agreement would. Disagreement demands attempts at honest, open conversation—even in those areas where we have felt ourselves compelled to say "no." We often entrench ourselves in the "no" only with great damage toward ourselves, and after a while that entrenchment becomes the easiest. That "no" through which our fathers fought their way becomes on our lips a complacency and a convention. In that sharp and clear "no" (which nevertheless does not exclude continuing conversation and does not hinder personal, even if at times painful, meeting), lies a far greater promise and blessing than in the gracious ignoring of each other because each shall have a right to believe as he wishes. A prefabricated and pharisaically limited judgment upon each other never leaves the door open to any conversation, because all is completely and absolutely decided in advance—and always to our own advantage. And if this ever did lead to a conversation, it would never amount to more than a poorly-disguised monologue that never dares venture forth from the trenches of apology and attack.

Even the greatest things in God's kingdom, even the truth of the gospel, even the confession of Christ and the right and true theology can become something false in our hands—in that very moment that we consider them as our possessions, as something we have and hold, and with which we elevate ourselves above our fellow men and fellow Christians. The same holds true between the churches, and thereby we lend support to the division. It is one thing to confess in obedience that truth which is given to us and which is bigger than we are, but it is a completely different thing to be, with self-satisfaction and pride, something in and of ourselves by virtue of that truth which is given to us. As with the good deeds that men have done and then looked upon as their own and which they then present before God and other men in such a way that they become evil and bad deeds, so it is with the churches and their truth. They thereby deny Christ as the only Lord and giver of life from whom men and churches receive all.

As the new man and the new fellowship is created through participation in the death of Christ and his resurrection, so that unity and that fellowship which makes up the church of Christ is created through participation in the death of Christ and his resurrection. For fellowship in the body of Christ is always fellowship in him that died and rose, for whom the way to life goes through death, in order that his Body should follow him on that way. This is also true of the churches' relationship to each other where the spirit of division has separated them from one another. Even that "no" which they must say to each other, can never be self-sufficient or pharisaical toward those who are considered to be "outside," for in the "no" to the other part there lies a relentless "no" to ourselves in our own isolationism and confinement, in our own churches' pride and self-glory. But this means that even the churches' relationship to each other within their mutual isolation and division shall be seen in the light of Christ's suffering and death for our sake and in the light of his victorious resurrection.

Only in that moment when we abandon subjectivism's and objectivism's homemade possibilities and dare to believe on Christ as the living Lord, and head of the body, the crucified, and risen, and ascended, which the body shall follow and obey, is a new way opened to us. The new way is not a broad superhighway, but a trail which at times may be hard to discover. There is more unity and fellowship on this small path than there is division, even in the midst of the "no." For that path, in the final analysis, is not our way but God's, who created us and redeemed us not to division but to fellowship.

Not only individuals have been freed that they might travel this path. So have the separate church communions —and also the Roman Catholic and the Evangelical Lutheran churches.

Chapter 2

THE TWO PARTIES

Two things characterize the reciprocal relationships among the denominations today. In the first place, deliberation is in progress within the individual confessions in which they seek to give an account of their own unique character in contrast with that of other groups. This brings about a tendency toward narrowness and isolation. But at the same time there is a movement which seeks an understanding of and cooperation with other denominations, such as the current ecumenical movement. Consequently we find at the same time a denominational, or confessional and a universalistic, or ecumenical movement. Though apparently in contradiction with each other, these two movements nevertheless strangely complement one another.

Where the first tendency gains the upper hand, we are threatened by a confessionalism which can have fatal consequences because the individual church isolates itself in its sacrosanct confession. Where the outward movement rules alone, we are in danger of an ecumenicity without content and without truth, which jumps over the difficulties and would reach the goal without hardship or seriousness. Logically, there is a contradiction between these two movements, and it cannot be denied that a strong tension can exist between them. But the history of the church is not all logical and does not proceed without tension.

These movements become irretrievably contradictory in the very moment we believe that mutual relationships between the confessions can be defined and regulated by human, theological means. If there is a glimpse today of a new way of relationship between various Christian communities, the reason is that something is happening in Christ's church which does not belong to theological considerations but is an expression of a new "salvation story" situation, where the Spirit has set men in motion with something that was not previously ripe for decision. Something can happen today which was not possible in previous centuries and which may actually take place through these apparently contradictory phenomena. Every "new era" has temptations and promises, danger and possibilities.

Both the "inward" and the "outward" movements which are taking place in the churches today stand under the banner of temptation and promise. The first can lead to isolationism and sectarianism, to self-opinionated and barren strife, just as the ecumenical can become a human effort for uniformity and a religious potpourri. Along these lines are found the temptations of the hour.

But it can also happen that the individual confession, through its renewal of the quest for the truth which once called it into being, constantly strives to be closer to Christ himself, the living Son of God. In this quest, the individual confession may at the same time relate itself toward other faith-communities in the conviction that Christ is not divided and in the faith that he as the living Lord also reveals his truth in other places than in one's own church. Along these lines can be found the promises of the hour.

In this situation the Roman Catholic and the Evangelical Lutheran churches meet one another. On the following pages we will try to sketch the meeting of these two as it takes place today. It must be conceded from the beginning that it is difficult if not impossible to describe the relationship between Roman Catholicism and Evangelical Lutheranism in abstract generalizations. We are not concerned here with two "isms," but rather with two church forms and understandings of Christianity, which are represented by living men in constant spiritual motion.

Neither the Roman church nor the Lutheran is the same today as it was four hundred years ago. Furthermore the relationship between them is not the same in different parts of the world because varied outer and inner circumstances have had their effect. There are differences in the purely "worldly sphere" where external sociological, political, economic, and other "all-too-human" circumstances play a role. Certainly these relationships in one way or another concern something important in the two forms of Christendom, and must not be underestimated; but it is not these variable circumstances in different countries and areas of the world which we will consider here. This is not a report as such but an experiment in arriving at theological opinion.

It is a peculiar fact that the Roman Catholic and Evangelical Lutheran Christendoms have never been able to disengage from each other. Note that even in the time of the Reformation these two parties are constantly battling each other: in part an often violent reciprocal repulsion, where there is talk of breach, of revolt, of apostasy, and of error; and in part, an awareness that Christ cannot be divided and that therefore the church of Christ is one. The

Evangelical church confessed and taught that the one, holy church is to continue forever. It was completely foreign for it to think of founding a new church. There can be only one church.

Even the Augsburg Confession is in itself an attempt to escape the breach which loomed as something disastrous for both parties. Melanchthon knew how serious it was that war had broken out in Christendom, and what significance it would have if that strife which had risen could be overcome and the disputing parties "brought back to one true accordant religion (as we are all subjects and soldiers under one Christ, so also we ought to confess one Christ . . .), and all things should be brought back to the truth of God, which with most fervent prayers we beseech God to grant." (*Preface to the Augsburg Confession.*)

But rupture between the two parties did occur in its incomprehensible mixture of necessity and blame, of truth and human confession. In the course of a few years the breach consolidated itself in the formation of theologically-limited church bodies which were differently defined in sociological, political, and cultural areas.

Nevertheless nothing has been able to erase either the bitterness of the breach and the vulnerability of their mutual relationship, or the awareness of the fate of being tied together and never being able to be free from each other. The Evangelical Lutheran and Roman Catholic problem has never been solved and never will be before God's hour. Behind all attempts to solve this riddle a mystery constantly lurks, and it will not allow itself to be clarified through theological interpretations—no matter how profound. In the midst of the most justified consciousness of the necessity of the breach—from the Protestant side—and, in the midst of the most convinced certainty that the breach was wrong—from the Roman side—there lies an unexplainable feeling of common fault and common fate. Thoughts on this never come to rest, either on the one side or the other. In an inexplicable manner they are tied together and orientated toward each other.

Where Lutheranism does not constantly hear a question posed to it by the Catholic church but considers the confessional question as solved and does not realize that it still is a burning problem, it is an unerring sign that it has become a stagnant church, ignorant not only of Catholicism but likewise of that for which Luther himself in the deepest sense longed and strove. And where the Roman church no longer—no matter how "hidden" this may be—is affected by the Reformation and does not hear the question put to it by the Reformation, it evades an issue with the result that sooner or later it blunders onto a sidetrack away from biblical truth and genuine Christian ground.

The attempts, polemic or irenic, during the course of centuries to explore and explain the problem of the cleavage of faith are countless. Let us name as examples three attempts to interpret the riddle which this split contains.

1. *The history of the human spirit.* Here the Reformation is seen essentially as a link in the development of the history of thought and in the evolution of spiritual ideas from the Middle Ages to the modern era. Actually the Reformation itself is still within the world of the Middle Ages and both its questions and its answers are to be understood within the context of the old time. Behind the Reformation lay something indicative of the future, still in swaddling clothes and unknown to the Reformers, and yet

clearly to be seen by those who read history with the perspective of subsequent centuries.

For this reason the essential nature and purpose of the Reformation does not appear in that which happens in the sixteenth century, but much later in the eighteenth and nineteenth centuries. That which is essential in Luther must be "distilled," so to speak, out of his words about sin, faith, and justification which are conceived in medievalism. All this belongs to "Protestantism from Above," a term used by Przywara, Catholic philosopher of religion, in contrast to the "Protestantism from Below," where the expressions and the ways of thinking of the Reformation are converted into a new form with new content, such as happened in the time of the Enlightenment. But the significant fact is that this new form germinates in the Reformation itself. This is very clearly expressed by the Protestant theologian, Ernst Troeltsch, when he says: "In its essential principles and expression, Protestantism is a transformation of medieval thought. That which is not medieval in it, e.g., modern thought (which it no doubt contains), enters the picture only after the primal and classic form of Protestantism has disintegrated and fallen apart." [1]

Instead of a religiosity that had its expression in the outer cults in obedience toward an external authority and an external organization in sacraments and priestly order, the attention is now directed inwardly toward the religious subject itself. As Troeltsch expresses it: "The inwardness, personality, and spirituality of religion; the autonomy, freedom, and totality of an ethic flowing from surrender to God." Briefly: The essential nature of the Reformation appears much later, most purely and clearly in that great philo-

[1] *Kultur der Gegenwalt,* I, IV, 1906 edition, pp. 25ff.

sophical movement which we call Idealism. In the battle
between the two great German theologians of the previous
century, Moehler the Roman Catholic, and Bauer the Protestant, this viewpoint plays a very large role. According
to Moehler it is specifically Idealism with its "inwardness,"
its "immediacy of God," its "subjectivism," where the focus
of significance (literally: center of gravity) is to be found
within the religious subject itself, which is the innermost
kernel of the Reformation. It is obvious, Moehler maintains, that Luther was quite unaware of this, even decidedly
against it, in what he personally desired and envisioned.
But it was implicit in his basic point of view, and according
to its own inner, irresistible logic had to be developed.

If this interpretation is correct, the battle of the Reformation must in the final analysis be considered an idle and
empty battle. According to this the Reformation is only an
intermediary stage leading toward later times, even on to
the newer Protestantism with its talk of "the Protestant
man," who is more or less released from every relationship
to the church.

In this way the Evangelical Lutheran church today is
confronted with a serious question which has not been given
a clear and conclusive answer and which cannot be dropped
with a mere twist of the wrist. Is the Reformation more
than a beginning to a constantly continued process of intellectual history? From the human point of view, the
future destiny of the Evangelical church is to be found in
its answer to this question.

If one would maintain that the Reformation is only a stage
in the process (i.e., a beginning which can be continued in-
definitely, the development of which is itself the most significant because of the constantly-created new forms of

Christianity in which every man has the right to arrive at his own Christian experiences by his own methods), then one must ask, what has actually happened to Christianity itself? Then Christianity is no longer a definite gospel which was given to the world, but is only a religious process which, with the historic Jesus as a point of reference, constantly receives its forms, philosophies, and points of view from the changing times.

It is one thing to say that Christianity must constantly renew itself in its forms of expression, in order that its message may reach our times and be understood as that which is vitally relevant. It is something completely different if one therefore concludes that Christianity is not in and of itself something definite, the apostolic gospel of Christ, which in its very essence is completely unchangeable from generation to generation. The new Protestant point of view has forgotten this. The question is: Have we not by this viewpoint approached in a strange manner the Roman doctrine of tradition with its talk of a continuous unfolding of Christian truth? Even though undeniably in another latitude!

There are plain signs in the Evangelical church today that it specifically does not propose to answer the question of the Reformation and the problem of the schism of the faith in this way. The Roman theologians are also turning from this interpretation. In spite of all respect for history and the development of history of thought, it must be maintained that this point of view has not recognized the essential question which was raised by the Reformation. Here the cleavage in the faith is in the last analysis made a harmless matter which can be explained by the interpreter who reflects on the past as a link in a necessary historical development. Here the solution is in far too high a degree dictated by the interpreter's own theological and religious attitude, and one must ask if this point of view is not itself, to a high degree, a transitional phenomenon. As an attempt to give an exhaustive interpretation of the mystery of the schism, it is unsatisfactory. It is one thing to see things in terms of the history of thought, but another to understand the Reformation as a genuine battle within the church where the real issue is not the development of human thought but the gospel of God's glory and grace, of faith, and of salvation.

2. *The history of religion.* History of religion often shows contradictions between two different types of religion: the institutional, cultic religion and the prophetic, personal religion. From this observation the contradictions between Evangelical Lutheran and Roman Catholic understandings of Christianity are seen as the contradiction which always exists within the religious life, as "the inner tension of religion itself" (Paul Tillich). From this point of view Romanism is seen as a religious form wherein the essential thing is the exterior solidity. This shows itself in the great weight laid upon the exterior visible authority, upon the cult with its sacraments and rituals, upon the holy orders, and upon tradition as the criterion of truth. The divine almost takes material form, and the entire inner religious life is tied to some very tangible externals. That which breaks into the tradition from the outside and causes disturbance and rupture is considered insurrection and error, against which the religious community must protect itself with every means. In contrast, Protestantism according to this view is a "prophetic" form of religion wherein there constantly comes a "word" from above. In this the deter-

mining factor is God's ever fresh invasion, that is both sovereign and free from all tradition, religious custom, and dogmatic forms. Here the "breach" with the concrete and "realized," with continuity and tradition, is seen as a witness to religious life and truth.

The German religious philosopher, Paul Tillich, has particularly sought to solve the confessional problems along these lines. Romanism is *Realisierung* and *Verwirklichung* in contrast to Protestantism as *Erschütterung* and *Durchbruch.* "Catholic" and "Evangelical" are therefore not as a matter of course synonymous with Roman Catholicism and Lutheran Christianity, but designate two basic types of the religious life which occur with more or less distinct form in every period of the history of Christianity, and which can be found within every religion. In this manner it is possible to find contrasts within Indian Bhakti religion and Buddhism which in their peculiar manner are similar to the contrasts between Romanism and Protestantism.

We will allow this brief account to be sufficient to indicate the direction which this type of thinking follows. But here we meet a strange and extremely interesting problem. It is clear that there is a kernel of truth in this viewpoint. There is in each religion, at any rate when each reaches a certain stage of its development, a certain tension between the static and tradition-bound, the fixed and immovable, and that which spontaneously breaks forth, the free and prophetic; between the cultural and the ethical; between tradition and new insights. Nor can it be denied that the relationship between Roman Catholicism and Protestantism contains a paradox which is peculiar to the religious life itself, as a tension between two positions that are counterpoints.

Confuses results & causes.

But as a description of the contrast between Roman Catholic and Evangelical Lutheran Christianity, this will not
suffice. If this were the whole truth, then there would not
be a real basis for a real separation of these two, for in that
case the contrasts between them would also be of a rela-
tively harmless character. It cannot be denied that the contrast here presented is a factor in the relationship between
the two parties as a kind of accompanying circumstance;
but to maintain that the contrast actually consists of this
would mean a disastrous setting aside of the essential concern of the Reformation, which was built wholly and completely on a theological and Christological plane, and
would mean a transferral of the problem to the plane of
general religion and religious psychology. That would
mean stating a problem which cuts across each of the two
parties individually and with which they actually are both
privately concerned as the determining and contrasting
relationship between them. The situation today within
these two church forms shows how careful one must be
with respect to establishing the contrasts on the plane of a
history of religion and psychology of religion. It is one
thing to recognize that basic differences in the understanding of Christianity can bring about consequences far out
in the psychological realm, far out in the practical concrete
practice of religion, and even out into the realm of religious
mentality and ideas. It is another thing to allow the contrast itself to consist of these things. For this reason this
attempt at interpretation, interesting and significant as it
may be, is not adequate.

3. *The primitive - Christian - dialectical interpretation.*
Closely related to this viewpoint is the "primitive-Christian-
dialectical" interpretation, which in one way only means

the same point of view taken back into primitive Christianity itself. We meet in this interpretation talk of the Petrine and the Pauline elements which represent two opposite factors in apostolic Christianity, which are related to each other as rest is to movement, as law to freedom, as the stable and palpable to the dynamic and spontaneous. The Petrine factor finds expression in the solid building, founded upon the rock, for a visible concrete authority with its "You are Peter, and on this rock I will build my church." Paul looked at it differently: not the exterior, visible structure, represented by the apostolic circles in Jerusalem, but the living word of God in every moment, the gospel of the free grace that needs no exterior apparatus as a guarantee with which to support itself, but where the Spirit in freedom constantly creates the conditions for the new life in the fulness of the spirit, in love's bondage to one's neighbor. The contrast between these two principles is mirrored concretely in the personal and tension-filled relationship between Paul and Peter, and the other great apostles, about which the first chapters of the letter to the Galatians especially give information. It is significant that in Luther's reading of this letter he constantly paralleled Paul's relationship to Jerusalem with his own relationship to Rome.

To this interpretation is added the Johannine concept of a synthesis which in the future, as the church of love, will transcend the contradictions between the Petrine and the Pauline. It should be remarked that the entire modern New Testament research has to no small degree shaken this rather schematic understanding of these two figures.

One can discern rather clearly in this interpretation that a certain speculative philosophy of history shines through, especially in the philosopher Schelling, who is one of the

spokesmen for this interpretation. This philosophy trans-
fers a characteristic of later history into an earlier context
of persons and relationships, in this case into the time and
persons of the New Testament.

Nevertheless this attempt at interpretation also contains
a truth and a relative legitimacy. For even though this
interpretation exaggerates and oversimplifies, it still cannot
be denied that this tension is to be found in the New Testament itself. Both the "Roman Petrine," and the "Pauline
evangelical" are to be found in a tension-filled unity, as
"complementary" truths, so to speak. And if we look further
at the course of history, upon the schism of faith and upon
the spiritual development of the Roman Catholic and Evangelical Lutheran, it can hardly be denied that there is a
kind of cultivation of Petrine and Pauline factors respec-
tively—an isolation of, and consequently a contrasting of,
two factors which belong together and must reciprocally
influence one another lest each of them degenerate into a
caricature of itself.

At the ecumenical meeting in Amsterdam in 1948, the
contradiction between "Catholic" and "Evangelical" came
to play a significant role in the definition of these two words
somewhat in terms of Petrine and Pauline. It was said that
this difference was the deepest and most essential between
the churches. In the debate that took place, it was maintained time and again that this strong emphasis upon the
contrast between "Catholic" and "Evangelical" was not
tenable. The church must at the same time be both "Catholic" and "Evangelical" because it must contain at the same
time both continuity and reformation. "Catholic" and "Evangelical" are not opposite concepts but "complementary concepts" that only possess their truth in their constant orienta-

tion toward each other. Here it is not necessary to separate, but to distinguish! If they are isolated from one another, they estrange themselves from the truth and cripple the understanding of what the Christian church is. If "Catholic" is isolated, we are in danger of taking refuge in a false objectivity where the truth is guaranteed by exterior things of cultal or doctrinal nature. If "Evangelical" is isolated, we are in danger of finding refuge in an equally false spiritualism and subjectivity.

What these three briefly discussed attempts at interpretation have in common is the theoretical, retrospective form in which they are conceived. Instructive and interesting as they may be, none of them has succeeded in explaining what it was that happened when the two parties went their own way. They point to interesting fragments, but the question itself remains unanswered. It simply cannot be answered along this way, because we are not here confronting only phenomena from "history of ideas" or "history of religion" but meeting something that has happened in the church of Christ, a combat that has broken out and a consequent division between believers. And this cannot be explained in terms of "history of ideas," "history of religion," or "psychology of religion."

There is more truth in the classical, theological-churchly interpretation where the contradictions are pictured polemically as contradictions between truth and lies, between true and false understandings of Christianity. The Reformation was an event in the church which from the Roman side is described as rebellion and breach, heresy and error. From the Lutheran side it is considered a breaking through of the truth of the gospel, as a triumph over the Roman perversion of Christianity, and as a renewal of Christ's church. The truth in this point of view is that here one does not take a stand outside the contradiction on top of a high ecclesiastical ivory tower, from which place one gains a view over the entire situation. Here one takes a stand and is personally engaged in the midst of the battle and the encounter. The truth lies in the understanding that one is a part of the struggle and that the struggle today also concerns truths and lies; that the question of the truth is just as burning today as it was in the time of the Reformation itself and a real meeting of the two parties is therefore necessary today also.

What is characteristic of the situation today is that something really does happen between the two parties. It is tempting to ask if there is any possibility at all for a conversation between these two—if there is actually (for those who are completely sober and have not fallen victim to some romantic visionaries) a way forward in this question. Doesn't everything in our time point to the fact that this relationship must be "abandoned"? We can point to the ever-stronger confessional consciousness of the Lutheran church, to the attitude different from the Romans which on the whole prevails in modern Protestantism toward church and Christianity, to the intolerance of the Roman church and its ever-repeated claim to be the only church, which contains within itself the whole truth, to its refusal to participate in the ecumenical work, as well as its position as a political power.

To this can be said that, in spite of these obvious things which really seem to exclude the possibility of a real conversation, something is occurring today in the mutual relationship of these two parties that perhaps opens the pos-

sibility for a meeting between them. This possibility has
not been seen since the time of the Reformation itself. In
spite of all these palpable facts, the two parties stand opposite one another not as two finished and sharply-defined
entities in a clear contrast to each other, but as two that
are entangled in an inevitable meeting, where the tension
between the "yes" and the "no" constantly separates them
only to bring them together again in the next moment. The
best of today's theological works dealing with the confessional question are borne by this living, dialectical tension
equally far from the earlier polemic and irenic theologies
which in the final analysis considered the question as answered and differed only in their interpretation of the
relationship.

We can point to Bible study as one of the most vital
points where something is actually happening between the
two parties. It is peculiar that one of the points where the
disagreement is the greatest and where the principal contrasts are most clearly seen can, in a given situation, become
a help to mutual conversation. To no small degree, this
has been the case in Roman Catholic and Evangelical Bible
exegesis in our time. One only needs note those works concerning biblical questions that are coming forth today from
both sides and the absolutely amazing agreement which
often exists between the scholars. And this agreement will
necessarily have gradually wider consequences. It will
follow that the two parties must look again at their dogmatic
heritage in the light of their renewed insight into the Word
of God. Both the Roman and the Lutheran church must
allow themselves to be tested by the message which they
meet in the Scriptures and they must take up with renewed
deliberation the great dividing points for a new considera-

tion—not only from their own studied confessional writings but in the light of a renewed study of the Bible.

Naturally the discussion arising out of a new biblical knowledge is still largely in the embryo stage, and is by no means a miraculous means to take the great dividing questions out of the world. Far from it. Nor is that the intention. But this is significant: To a much greater degree than before—and this among other things is to be credited to the historical-critical research method—the two parties go about the task of reading the Bible without their confessional spectacles and without constantly squinting at their doctrinal prejudices. In the light of the Bible's witness to God's revelation both parties will be forced to give account of what they mean by their terms. This can eventually mean a clarification of the concepts and can be a help in the destruction of prejudice, and in freeing words from a tradition-bound, almost invincible, and often very unpleasant meaning.

A significant document in this matter is Pope Pius XII's Bible Encyclical of September 30, 1943, *Divino Afflante Spiritu.*

Without doubt this entire question, which can only be mentioned here, will make possible an even more fruitful meeting of the two parties in the future than is possible today.

But still other factors must be mentioned. The first is a more exterior, sociological factor. In the course of the last 150 years the relationship between the two parties has gradually changed. In the Middle Ages, Roman Catholicism had undisputed sovereignty. There was so to speak only one room, using this word with a historical, sociological meaning. Then came the time of the Reformation with its

violent battles which reached their temporary conclusion
with the religious peace of 1555. Western Europe then
existed in two great, separated rooms, literally speaking: to
be a Roman Catholic or a Protestant did not mean simply
to have a different faith but also to have a different terri-
tory, different politics, different culture, even different economic principles. Interaction between the two was not
great and the various rulers were on guard so that contacts
might be as few as possible.

This purely exterior separation of rooms provided the
conditions necessary for a purely Roman Catholic development of culture which took place in the seventeenth century: the so-called Baroque culture, the last form of a
purely Roman Catholic development of culture which was
determined to no small degree by the Counter Reformation and the Jesuit order.

With the Enlightenment came a change. Then "the
rooms were mixed." The severe contradictions were made
relative; a less polemic, more tolerant, attitude came forth.
At the time that the two confessions were separating men
even more from each other theologically, purely human
and cultural values were drawing them more closely together. Tolerance tears down many walls.

In Romanticism a sphere of culture was created which
was shared by both Romans and Protestants. A few of the
leading personalities of Romanticism went over to Roman
Catholicism; however it is not possible to maintain that
Romanticism was a Roman Catholic culture-movement.
It does mean that Romans and Protestants were then
pulled closer together in one room, so that the difference
between them was not as marked as before in culture,
politics, etc., but was more and more a purely religious dif-

ference. In the light of this understanding, we can say that this development has continued, so that today we find Romans and Protestants united in one human room. Within this context, spiritual struggles take place not only between these two but also between other religious and anti-religious points of view.

Another thing that has contributed toward changing the relationship between Romanism and Protestantism today is the fact that much water has run under the bridge since the Reformation. At that time the Evangelical church confronted a Catholicism that in many ways was weak, a Catholicism that only to a slight degree could realize its ideals, where human failings had penetrated too far both into its head and its members. This gave the young Evangelical church a certain triumphant undertone. Now the Evangelical church has become, if not old, at least a rather adult church. And a not altogether glorious history lies behind it. Now it also knows what apostasy, inertia, and falsity are. It has also arrived, in its own way, infinitely far away from that which was its intention, its idea, to use Karl Adam's expression. It seems to us that dark clouds fall across the Roman church through the centuries, but those clouds fall equally darkly over the Evangelical Lutheran church. Now the two may at least meet in a kind of a solidarity of sinfulness, and that is not always a poor place to meet, even for two churches.

Common need has brought the two parties into very real contact with one another. A German Catholic names three things that are significant as far as the Germans are concerned: the prisons and concentration camps of the Nazis; the war and its boundless physical and spiritual need; and after the war the frightening refugee problem

resulting from millions of people being forced to abandon
their homes and take up residence in completely different
parts of the country. Then Roman churches had to be used
for Evangelical worship and Evangelical for Roman. There
they were pulled together by common confession and faith.
Where there is need, something can happen for which
satiety does not feel compulsion and which satiety does
not allow. Mighty forces now break forth upon the earth.
It cannot be denied that we have entered in upon an
epoch[2] of an absolutely unique magnitude, a time when
much of the old collapses and something new is born. During such times something also happens to the old antago-
nisms. Then walls can fall down that previously seemed
indestructible. The new time that is breaking forth will
not be without influence upon the relationships between
Roman Catholicism and Protestantism.

   In relation to this, one thing more must be mentioned:
the change in the "spiritual climate." Here we encounter
a point that must be discussed with the greatest care, since
the facts by no means speak one clear language; in fact,
they give most often an extremely dim picture. (It is possible that the following is true primarily of the European
conditions and does not have any validity in other places.)
With this reservation, there is indeed talk of a development
whose reality is not denied from either side. There are
signs on both sides of a new frame of mind that will make
it possible to consider the confessional question in a completely new manner. This is significant, for it cannot be
denied that in the course of time a different method of
interpreting what is religious has been created. Not only
do the different Christian questions receive different an-

----

[2] *Tidehverv:* the name of crisis theology in Denmark.

swers but the difference crops out even in the way that the questions are posed. Through the centuries, by many invisible ways, almost insurmountable prejudices have been formed, often knit to very specific terms and dogmatic concepts. The almost magical power of such terms acts as a conditioned reflex in releasing certain specific reactions, which may be unaccompanied by an attempt to understand what the counterpart intends by the terms. One forgets that in the course of time words can receive other meanings and today may express something completely different from that which they originally meant.

There is need on both sides for basic work in clarifying. There is hardly a concept not in need of revision. First and foremost it is necessary to seek to find the intention of the word used, not only in its historic understanding but also as the word is used today. There are signs that many of the old prejudices are falling. And thereby a very basic hindrance for a meeting between the two parties is being removed.

Here we must add a few words about confessional toleration. For the sake of clarity, we must distinguish between toleration on the civil and on the theological plane. Civil toleration is a good which must absolutely be respected. The two parties must find on the common-human plane the best possible method of living together. Anything else would be completely indecent. Religious persecution, hindrance of free worship of God, and the prevention of spiritual self-expression are not reconcilable with those rights which we owe to each other as fellow men.

It is wholly disgraceful and degrading for the two parties, as well as damaging for the church and its work, to confront one another as two political powers where power at the same time means suppression of the other party. A political Christianity, understood in this way, has from the outset judged itself; but it is not an unknown phenomenon even today! This is one side of the matter, and about this there ought not for one moment be any disagreement by either of the two groups. Each ought on its own consider it an honor to extend to the other, without reflection, that same freedom it desires for itself. The Evangelical command that what we wish others to do unto us we ought also to do unto them, applies in an unqualified way also on the confessional scene. But this does not mean and can never mean that the battle over the truth should be discontinued.

It is true that the various confessions have consolidated themselves as secure institutions with definite borders. Even in the time of the Reformation they were actually defined by the various territories, so that each principality had its established confession. In this context there is something static and almost purely civil in the term "confession." But in this word "confession" something else can also be found—a witness of truth and of faith which cannot be shut up within a confession that has imprisoned itself in a static definition of a once-living truth. Confession in the real sense of the word is something spiritually alive. Thus understood, no confessional peace can be found. That wound which was suffered because of the Reformation was not to be healed by the conceiving of confessions, but is ever open—equally open today as it was in 1517 when Luther nailed his 95 theses on the cathedral door in Wittenberg—as living as on that day when Luther received the papal bull of excommunication, and burned it!

The standpoint of confessional peace cannot be taken

seriously because it does not recognize that the issue here is not solved merely by civilly allowing the other to live in peace and by an attitude of mutual "respect." There will always be strife concerning the truth of the gospel. To this, the Bible, early Christianity and the entire history of the church also witness. A genuine respect for each other will of itself lead into conflict, because genuine respect takes the other point of view so seriously that it is worthy of combat and refutation.

An ecumenical theology must not become a theology without sharp teeth and without face. It cannot be content with a mere ascertainment and listing of differences and resemblances in its escape from the perhaps extremely painful encounter with its opponent. Without losing itself and becoming a completely harmless undertaking, ecumenical conversation cannot become a theology without passion, without "anger." If tolerance is to signify a theology of this sort, then theological tolerance is a contradiction in terms. A theological confessional tolerance must mean a demand for objectivity and impartiality, for openness and sensitivity; for sober work in trying to understand the opponent and what he says, and for unrestricted readiness to give an account of one's own point of view. There is a difference between a churchly, confessional Pharisaism which in advance has a monopoly on the truth, and a theology which does not make compromises and which in a given moment lays "politeness" aside and does make attack. This can and ought to happen in a full, personal recognition of one's opponent.

The Evangelical Lutheran theologian has no right to doubt that the Roman Catholic church has very important questions to pose, and he must seek to answer these questions in all sincerity. At times there is a certain arrogance among Protestant theologians who seem to have confidence in the conviction that the Lutheran church possesses the entire biblical, evangelical truth in contrast to the apostate Roman church. This triumphant condescension is not becoming. It must not be forgotten that many things look different today than they did at the time of the Reformation. But at the same time we can also find in the Evangelical camp a peculiarly weak, almost fearful and submissive behavior, which is not worthy or genuinely ecumenical.

The Evangelical theologian ought to expect the Roman Catholic theologian to listen to those questions that are raised by the Evangelical church. Without any suggestion of self-righteousness (would it really be possible today?), the Evangelical theologian must pose one central question for his opponent. The final and determining question concerns whether or not the entire development of Roman dogma, including its later phases, and its mighty ecclesiastical structure truly gives to the gospel itself the central place from which all else receives its definite and significant place. The Evangelical church must, if it is to be a genuinely evangelical church, be aware that to an equally high degree this question pertains also to itself. This does not detract from the fact that it is duty bound, through attentiveness to every question from the Roman church, to pose the same question as incisively and as urgently to the Roman Catholic church. Whether or not this will be heard is not its concern. In this way ecumenical conversations can have an incisiveness and an absolute earnestness which have their model in the times of the New Testament and the Reformation themselves, where the question of the truth of the gospel in contrast to falsification and error constantly came forth. But it can happen that, even where contradictions appear most violently, unity is closer than one believes, closer at any rate than where one in sheer confessional politeness and agreement actually avoids the other.

Ecumenical conversation has its own laws. It must be conducted both in truth and in love. It cannot be denied that the conversation has sometimes deteriorated into a certain indifference toward demands for the truth, where agreement has been sought in an ethereal stratum beyond the objective and stern demand for mutual respect for the truth, or where the conversation has been limited to considering practical cooperation without regard to teachings or faith.

Ecumenical conversation today knows it must be bound to the truth. When the two parties meet, the goal is not to create a compromise or to procure a cheap dogmatic unity by each giving up that which offends the other party the most. Neither has a right to demand that the other party shall renounce a tittle of what it has confessed as the truth, and neither has the right to give up any of that truth which has been entrusted to it. And both will know that they are under obligation to the truth itself. In real ecumenical conversation there is always a "third." The conversation consists not merely of a two-sided exchange where attention is fastened on one's own position, but of a much deeper exchange where both parties together have their view directed toward the third party of the conversation—the truth itself. Without the presence of this "third" the conversation becomes as salt which has lost its savor. It is a joy to see and experience how ecumenical discussions, includ-

ing discussions between Protestants and Romans, have
gained in profundity and objectivity because the perspective has been broadened and deepened.

Ecumenical conversation takes place in love; that is, in
mutual respect and sincere openness, in which one thinks
well about one's neighbor and construes all according to
its best meaning, but does not on the other hand allow
one's neighbor to live in peace because that is most comfortable. Love does not seek its own. It does not rigidly
take a stand on its own merit, but "rises above itself" in
order to meet the other. It does not meet the other with a
preconceived distrust, but in confidence. It does not allow
any possibility for mutual understanding to be lost, and
preserves hope until the last.

With the two parties sufficiently presented for the time
being, the conversation between them can begin.

Chapter 3

SCRIPTURE AND TRADITION

There is a problem that has frequently been the subject of bitter debate between the Romans and the Protestants ever since the Reformation. It is today one of those points where the difference between them appears most clearly and where there is need for a high degree of objective and unprejudiced consideration. This is the question of scripture and tradition. This may sound dry and discouragingly theological to many, but actually it is not. Here we are immediately in the midst of the conflict.

One of Grundtvig's hymns says, in effect: "Our faith is not in just anything that one calls Christian." Christianity has a content, but not just any content. Roman and Evangelical Christianity are agreed upon this, and on this point they have a common front against a subjective and individualistic view of Christianity which, in principle, allows every man freely to form his own understanding of what Christianity is. But they are not agreed upon what the faith receives its content from.

First the Roman point of view: As the sources of the faith, the Roman church looks toward two things, scripture and tradition—or more correctly, tradition and scripture. For before the scripture comes the tradition, that is, the oral teachings of the apostles. Before the scriptures was

the church, founded by Jesus himself, as a definite, visible
society, with the apostles, particularly Peter, as leaders and
highest authorities. "He who hears you, hears me," Jesus
had said, and he had therewith given these human instruments a unique significance in his church. And this unique
position was handed down as an inheritance directly to the
bishops and particularly to the successors of Peter in the
bishop's office in Rome. To be sure the time of the apostles
is unique, and the Roman church maintains that the revelation concludes with them; and yet not all is thereby said.
Down through the history of the church a steady unfolding
of the content of the revelation takes place, a constant
clarification of its content. In the early church much was
still in embryonic form; there was still much that was not
present at all in the consciousness of the believers, but
which receives its development later in the life of the
church.

All this takes place in the tradition, that is, in the life of
the church in its various forms: the witness of the fathers,
the liturgy, the pastoral letters of the bishops, the catechisms, the writings of the saints and the great theologians,
but first and foremost in the decisions of the synods and
in the popes' infallible utterances. Tradition is a living
stream down through the church, and this living tradition
is the first and foremost source of the faith.

This should not be understood as meaning that every
tradition which appears in the church is a source of faith.
There can be traditions that drop away by themselves,
traditions that do not have an obligatory character, even
traditions that are cut off because on closer examination
and trial they prove to be inconsistent with the church and
its teachings. Tradition in its genuine meaning exists only

where the church itself through its divinely instituted means fixes, recognizes, and defines this or that as true tradition. Here the pope plays an extremely significant and completely decisive role. When the pope speaks in his capacity as the foremost leader of the church, he speaks infallibly, and that which he says does not stand by virtue of anything but his infallible authority—neither by strength of its proof through the Bible nor by strength of the ratification by the church.

But the Bible is also to be found in the Roman church. What is the Roman Catholic view of it? These writings (we refer to the twenty-seven books of the New Testament) are in the first place later than the tradition, later than the church. Scripture contains only a very limited part of the teachings of the early apostles, which for the most part were not even written down but were spread through the church by oral delivery. That the church precedes the scripture is most plainly shown in the simple fact that the church established which writings belong to Holy Scripture, and which shall be canon, that is, the rule for the church.

None of the New Testament writings contain in and of themselves the sign of divine inspiration, but it is the church that has decided what these writings are and that they shall be acknowledged as inspired by God and therefore as infallible. To be sure, these writings have a completely unique place in the life of the church and are an inexhaustible source for edification and teaching. But the Bible can never be the only source of faith—let alone the rule of faith. It must always be understood and interpreted in accordance with the tradition. None may venture to interpret scripture contrarily to that meaning which the church has always given to these words, for only the church can judge concerning the true meaning and understanding of the Holy Scriptures. From the outset, it is impossible that there should ever arise a contradiction between these. All later tradition is only a further development of what is embryonic in the New Testament, almost in the same manner as all mathematics evolves from a few basic mathematical axioms. Scripture and tradition are both given by the same Holy Spirit and ought therefore, as the Council of Trent expresses it, to be acknowledged and honored with the same pious veneration.

This conception of the relationship between scripture and tradition is in contrast to the Evangelical understanding. This became evident as early as the Reformation when, for example, Luther soon found himself in contradiction with the tradition of the church. At the disputation with John Eck in 1519, Luther was forced to maintain that the ecumenical councils and the pope cannot be the highest authority in the question of salvation where these do not have the Bible and its witness on their side. Luther believed that whatever is contrary to the Bible is a perversion of Christianity, and he declared that both the council and the popes had made mistakes. Beside the Apostles' Creed, he kept the old symbols of the early church, not by strength of the tradition of the church or its authority, but out of the conviction that these had not established new doctrines but only combated false interpretations.

On Evangelical grounds there developed a pronounced skepticism with respect to the concept of tradition which essentially became synonymous with human invention, fabrication, and distortion. In one of Bunyan's works, he tells of "Mr. Tradition" who together with "Mr. Human-

Wisdom" and "Mr. Human-Invention"—"proper men of courage and of skill"—are the devil's obviously capable helpers in the struggle against the fortress "Mansoul"—a strong but true picture of the Puritan suspicion of the tradition. It is also characteristic that one cannot find in the subject index of the Lutheran confessional writings an entry under "tradition," except a reference to "man-made rules" and under this there is only a discussion of customs and usages, of ceremonies and worship rituals and church laws; that is, those things that belong to the periphery of the Christian life and which can have no central significance.

The word tradition has lost its essentially theological weight and plays no role for faith itself. There is only one source of faith, not two, and that is Holy Scripture, which contains the entire apostolic witness concerning Jesus Christ. To this there can never be added anything else, as therein everything has been said that is necessary for life and blessedness. Beside scripture, and previous to the written word in its basic content, stands the Apostles' Creed, the shortest and clearest expression for the original Christian confession. Whatever is added to these two basic sources can never have obligatory significance for faith and Christian life.

The Evangelical church will not deny that tradition arises nor does it deny that it may have its importance, but it is always secondary to scripture. It is true that the Reformers were eager to maintain their agreement with the church fathers and to prove that certain Roman customs and teachings are later additions. But they always distinguished sharply between the norm—which has essential authority—and what was only derivative and had authority only insofar as it was in accord with the Holy Scriptures. We cannot call this tradition *and* scripture, but must title it scripture *alone*. It cannot be said that scripture must be interpreted according to the tradition of the church—but rather that the Scriptures with the Creed are the essential and, in the final analysis, the only authority and norm, according to which all later tradition is to be judged.

We shall not consider here the vital question of the relationship between the Scriptures and the Apostles' Creed, which has played a large role within the Lutheran church, particularly in Denmark. Both those who place the most weight on the Scriptures and those who acclaim the Apostles' Creed are agreed that whatever lies beyond these two can have no binding significance for the Christian church.

Let this be sufficient for the present as a characterization of the two views. It may appear that the contradictions between them are irreconcilable and that not least on this point has the struggle between the Romans and the Evangelicais been both burning and uncompromising. We could now review the various phases of that struggle and enter into the often extremely shrewd and logical explanations and polemical results which in the course of time have been undertaken by both sides. We could see how the Roman church has maintained that the Evangelical point of view is both illogical and has led to the wildest type of arbitrariness because it lacks an established principle of authority which can say to every age the final word on how scripture shall be interpreted and understood. And on its side, the Evangelical church could point to the consequences of the Roman principle of tradition whereby dogmas which cannot with any justification be said to belong to scripture or to the early church are now demanded as necessary for salvation, and whereby the church has usurped a power and an authority in questions of faith which belong only to God.

This would naturally be very interesting, but we leave this pursuit, partly because it would become altogether too extensive and partly because it is very doubtful that we would progress a single step thereby. We will therefore seek to approach the question in another way in order to see more clearly where the contradiction lies, and, if possible, make a little progress toward mutual understanding. Let us pose the question purely historically, looking to the earliest beginnings of Christianity in order to see how this difficult problem arose.

If we seek to understand how this problem developed in the primitive church, we must greatly modify this briefly presented Evangelical understanding of tradition. For it is a fact that the oral gospel or the tradition plays an extraordinarily central role in these earliest times.

In the first place, it is interesting to see how much the religious milieu into which Christendom came was ruled by the concept of tradition. The late Jewish piety lived by the law, Torah, both that which was written down and that which was orally delivered. The orally-delivered was of equally divine origin as the written. Moses had received the law directly from God and had written down a part of it, while a part was conveyed further by oral means. It was the scribes, the rabbis, who were the bearers of the oral tradition. A rabbi once sought to convince his disciples concerning a certain interpretation of the law. They did not become convinced by his arguments until he informed them that an earlier rabbi had also held the same interpretation. In this manner they were convinced. Tradition was

the criterion of truth. A Jewish work seeks to establish all
the links of the delivery right back to Moses. There is a
reasonably close parallel between this Jewish-rabbinical
concept of the relationship between scripture and tradition
and the Roman Catholic concept.

But it is also of great importance to see where Jesus
stands in regard to tradition. Jesus entirely dismisses the
oral tradition as being made up of human additions. Several
times he refers directly to the written word as God's own
word but it appears clearly in the accounts of the evan-
gelists that he considers himself as Lord also over the
written word for only he, as Son of the Father and as the
Messiah, knows what the content of the law is. He thereby
draws upon himself the hatred and the fury of the scribes,
because he independently, authoritatively, and completely
without regard to the interpretations of the scribes and the
rabbis, i.e., the tradition, reads and understands the Old
Testament. Here was that One who was greater than tradition and scripture. Here was he who was the fulfilment of
the often obscure and unclear words of the Bible.

A new tradition now develops in the early church no
longer with the law as content but with the living Christ
as its content. Before a line of the New Testament was
written, there was a confession of Christ, the apostolic
kerygma, which was spread further through oral proclamation. To be sure there was a scripture which was of in-
estimable importance, namely the writings of the Old
Testament. These were thoroughly read and studied, but
now after the resurrection of Christ, they were seen in an
entirely new light. They were no longer read with the
eyes of the rabbis but in the light of all the great events
which had taken place in Christ. Christ was found through-

out the old books. The new was not to be found written in any book. It had *happened,* and now this was to be proclaimed from man to man. Here oral delivery did truly play a tremendous role.

What was the content of what they handed down? It was partly the circumstances of the life of Jesus, partly the words of Jesus, both the individual and the collected, but specifically it was the witness to Christ based on the main events of the Savior's life. We can read about this for example in I Corinthians 15:3ff, Philippians 2:6ff, I Timothy 3:16. We already meet in the primitive church the most significant links in the Apostles' Creed. In contrast to Jewry where the rabbis were the bearers of the tradition, it was the apostles in young Christianity who were the focal points in the delivery. They were instruments of the Holy Spirit himself, which through them formed and shaped that message which proclaimed salvation in Christ.

It was further a unique fact that not only was Christ the content of the tradition, but he was also the living Lord who was operative in the oral proclamation. It was surely a doctrine, and yet the content was not only a teaching but a living Lord. There was in the tradition always something that was greater than the tradition itself. It was not only a new law, a new teaching, and a new concept of God which was the content of that delivery, but something that was far greater: Christ himself. He was always the Lord of the tradition.

If we are therefore to ask how the gospel of Jesus Christ was heard and spread in these first times, the answer must be: through oral tradition where those men who had been especially commissioned as apostles proclaimed the message to those who followed them. Through many years there was preaching and baptism and celebration of the Eucharist before the congregations received a collection of the gospels and apostolic letters as a permanent expression of the voice of the apostles from the early days when foundations were being laid.

From this brief and summary presentation, it will appear that there was actually a time when the tradition truly played a very essential role, not only in the periphery, but in the very center of the Christian life. The congregation was, as Luther at one time said, not a "pen house" but a "mouth house." Before there was scripture, there was oral tradition; before there was a New Testament, there was a church; before men wrote, they spoke, they confessed, they baptized, and they held Holy Communion.

In the midst of this living, oral witness, in the midst of the life of this early church, our New Testament arose. It was not long before both the words of Jesus and the events of his life were written down. Our gospel accounts are really nothing but the written deposit of that which had previously lived in the oral tradition. First Mark, then Matthew, and Luke. This entire process, whose development is extremely complicated, we shall not pursue further here. It is a fact that there arose a scripture and that this scripture has a distinct character. It closes and dams up the stream, so to speak. It is the state's evidence concerning the first apostolic proclamation, concerning the time of the laying of foundations, which is different from every later time because it is here that the testimony to Christ is created. This first period is in one sense not a link in the tradition, because it stands at the very fountainhead of the tradition.

A contradiction between oral tradition and scripture

could not be imagined. They did after all flow from the same spring. Scripture was the deposit of the apostolic voice which was heard in the primitive church and behind which stood the living Lord himself. But it is decisive to distinguish between those first times and all subsequent periods. No pope, no bishop, no reformer, no inspired prophet is or can ever become an apostle. When the church in the first centuries gathered together the writings of the New Testament and made a choice from the many different writings that existed in the church, it acknowledged itself the difference between that first period of establishment and all later times. By the establishment of these writings as canon, a factual curtailment was accomplished in the stream of the tradition in the fact that it was thereby declared that every later tradition was to be judged and measured by that first apostolic tradition which had laid the foundation.

Let us turn back to our original question of the contradiction between the Roman Catholic and the Evangelical Lutheran view regarding the relationship between scripture and tradition. First of all there is something here on which the two parties are agreed. They are both confessional churches, that is to say, churches that acknowledge Jesus as Christ and Lord, whose focal point is not one or another "historical" Jesus to whom it should be possible to reach with the help of historical research, but whose center is that Christ whom the apostles confessed and concerning whom their creed and scripture bear witness. Neither the Roman Catholic nor the Evangelical church will acknowledge a tradition in which Christ is not called Lord. In short: both churches would be apostolic in the sense that both would build on that same fundamental that the apostles laid and which they in their persons represented. If there were not this common basis, a conversation between them would from the outset be impossible and absolutely fruitless.

Here we have reached that point where our paths part. We begin again with the Roman viewpoint in the hope that we can now elaborate upon what we said at the beginning. The Roman church acknowledges in its theology the decisive difference between that first period of the founding of the church and subsequent periods insofar as it maintains that the revelation was concluded with the last of the apostles. And yet there is something in its view that again annuls this distinction. The Roman Catholic Church distinguishes between a *traditio passiva,* that is, a "treasury of faith" which shall pass down through all ages without changing, and a *traditio activa,* which constantly unfolds the changeless treasury of faith. It constantly elaborates and develops the content of faith in richer measure, allowing truths not seen before to come to the light of day.

Karl Adam, the well-known Roman theologian, says in his book, *The Spirit of Catholicism,* "We Catholics acknowledge readily, without any shame, nay with pride, that Catholicism cannot be identified simply and wholly with primitive Christianity, nor even with the Gospel of Christ, in the same way that the great oak cannot be identified with the tiny acorn. There is no mechanical identity, but an organic identity. And we go further and say that thousands of years hence Catholicism will probably be even richer, more luxuriant, more manifold in dogma, morals, law and worship than the Catholicism of the present day. A religious historian of the fifth millennium A.D. will without difficulty discover in Catholicism conceptions and forms and practices which derive from India, China and Japan, and he will have to recognize a far more obvious 'complex of opposites.'" [1]

There is in the church a living and creative consciousness of faith or a faith instinct which presses onward, and is a creative life power. It is a power which might be called the living spirit of revelation. This creative and active tradition is not a development out in the blue but is primarily under direction and discipline through the infallible hierarchical authority, that living and authoritative voice that is heard through the mouth of the pope and the entire ecclesiastical doctrinal teaching. That tradition which is recognized and formed under the direction of the church is Christ's own voice on every point in the life of the church. Tradition can be compared with a constantly flowing stream directed by the Holy Spirit himself. The church is actually the extension of the living Christ himself.

For that reason the tradition is infallible. What we said about Christ as the Lord of the apostolic tradition is equally true in the same immediate manner down through all history. The sovereignty of Christ in the tradition is to be found very simply in the fact that this tradition is the extension of Christ himself.

What role does scripture play in this view? As far as I can see, there is no consistent clarity at this point in the Roman church. There are voices that completely incorporate scripture as a link in the tradition, even though it does have a particular place as the first link. The main emphasis is then decisively placed upon the tradition as the contemporary authoritative voice of the doctrine-teach-

[1] *The Spirit of Catholicism* (Image Book, Garden City, N. Y.: Doubleday & Co., 1954), p. 2.

ing hierarchy. On the question of what the content of the faith is, scripture is not able to give decisive and satisfactory information. In the first place, truth cannot be contained within a book and, in the second place, scripture is neither clear nor consistent but must be interpreted and understood from the contemporary, living voice óf the tradition.

Other voices give scripture a precedence over all later tradition and hold that tradition can only contain that which already lies within scripture, which is in this manner made normative for all tradition of later periods. This can never be identified with the wider continuing consciousness of faith in the church. We here come to a point that has not been clarified in Roman theology despite the fact that in later years a great deal has been written about this. For our purposes it is sufficient only to note this nuance, which is not without interest for Evangelical theology, as it naturally will seek association with the last indicated point of view. In the meantime no matter how great the interest in Bible study in the Catholicism of our day, it must be said that the decisive weight continues to fall upon the tradition. This becomes especially obvious in the declaration of the dogma of Mary's physical ascension of 1950 that has no reasonable basis either in scripture or in the tradition of the first centuries. Here a truth of faith necessary for salvation has been based upon the active, creative tradition alone.

It is here that Evangelical protest intrudes with its question. The Evangelical church must also acknowledge the concept of tradition. We all live in tradition. That belongs to the condition and structure of human life. That is true in the community, in culture, in the family, and in the

individual life. Without tradition, life would lose its continuity. It would be uprooted and would soon disintegrate.
That is true in a purely sociological and individual-
existential consideration and it is also true in the religious
and Christian realms. There is something that is received
from earlier generations which is appropriated and transformed and which is passed on to the next generation. We
are all links in the tradition, whether or not we wish to be
and whether or not we are aware of it. There is also something that is called a Lutheran tradition, a Reformed, a
pietistic, a modernistic tradition, etc. This is true of worship life and its various forms and expressions, it is true
of theology, and it is also true within the work of interpreting the Bible. We do not stand "alone" with the Bible
without anything further being added, but we always add
our understanding to it and this is to a high degree dependent upon our "tradition." In the very manner that we
understand and interpret the Bible we are dependent upon
previous generations. In the ecumenical movements of our
day we have received a sharper insight into the different
traditions, that is, the different interpretations of Christianity
represented by the different denominations, and are experi-
encing more than at any previous time a strange interaction
between the various traditions.

But it is necessary to speak about tradition not only in
this sense. In what is most central, in the gospel itself
and in the administration of the sacraments, there is also
talk of tradition. There is truly something that is received,
is appropriated, and is passed on. There is a tradition of
preaching, there is a worship tradition in the gathering of
the congregation with whose ever-recurring liturgical forms
as we know them from Baptism and Holy Communion.

And not least, there is the handing down of the confession of Christ in the Apostles' Creed which takes place at every baptism. This has been pointed to with great power by Grundtvig in Denmark. The Evangelical church neither can nor will deny that there is tradition both in a broader and a narrower meaning.

Is there then in the final analysis any difference between the Roman and the Evangelical churches on this point? Is it not possible to work our way through to a reconciliation of the two viewpoints? Is the "no" of the Evangelical church so unyielding and decisive on this point as it would appear to be, judging from battles of previous times? Why does not the Evangelical church acknowledge in obedience and gratefulness the Roman view that tradition truly is the living voice of Christ, which apparently has never been broken, and is encompassed and born, secured and guaranteed, by the infallible authority of the hierarchy? Why not submit to the obvious finality, authority, clarity and apparently effective strength which accompanies this view of tradition?

Here it must be said very distinctly that the Evangelical church cannot do this. Here in spite of everything it must speak a decisive "no." Here we are concerned with the very heart of the matter in the Evangelical view. Evangelical Christianity lives in tradition as well as Roman. But it has a different view of the relationship between tradition and scripture than does the Roman. It revolves about an entirely different understanding of what it means to say that Christ is the Lord of the tradition. This is after all the question: Who is Lord in the tradition? Is it Christ or is it—perhaps completely hidden and camouflaged—man himself? Is it the sovereign word of God which in its freedom and superiority rules—or is it perhaps the pious, very religious, very believing church.

When the question is asked in this manner, it is important to stress that it is asked of both Roman and Evangelical churches. Each church is under the temptation to make itself the lord of the tradition or, expressing it differently, to allow its own tradition to take supremacy over the living and acting word of God, to interpret the witness of scripture concerning the living God in his work of salvation in terms of itself and its own tradition. The Evangelical church is subject here to as equally great a temptation as the Roman and has often fallen into that temptation.

A "Lutheran" tradition or a "modern" tradition will probably guard against calling itself infallible, for that would after all be "Catholic"! But that does not exclude the possibility that they nevertheless may assume their tradition to be sacrosanct. Without actually saying it, they may declare their own tradition infallible—no councils or solemn declarations are needed for that! But in this way each one becomes the lord of the tradition, whether it is one or another form of theological orthodoxy or liberalism, whether it is a Lutheran conception of scripture, or whether it is the free, religious man who himself completely "untraditionally" creates his own religious convictions. Our shadows follow us!

That which is a temptation for the Evangelical church, and to which it has time after time succumbed, has in a way become the officially-established fact and rule in the Roman Catholic church. It is tradition that has the final word. It is the church with its infallible doctrine which has become the final court of appeal in correct understanding and exposition of scripture.

The Evangelical point of view may be sketched in this manner: Before the New Testament existed—the church existed. The apostles did not receive a command to write, but to proclaim, to baptize, and to celebrate the Eucharist. The church is not based upon a book but upon a living witness, upon an act of God. The church is the people of God created and maintained through the proclamation of the apostles, through Baptism and through Holy Communion. It was through those means that the Holy Spirit himself acted and worked. In this church from the very beginning there was the book of the old covenant which was understood and proclaimed on the basis of all that which had happened in Christ. And out of this church came the book of the new covenant with its witness to Christ in the gospel accounts as well as in the letters of the apostles. In addition, there was the creed which was heard at baptism and which from the very beginning summed up the apostolic proclamation. It was the confession that one received at the beginning of instruction for baptism and which one "gave back" directly before the solemn moment of the baptism.

At the moment when the living voices of the apostles are no longer to be heard, but when the church and its tradition continues to live, the apostolic witness in its writings and confession receives a completely unique place and significance. Now there is meaning in saying that scripture is absolutely superior to tradition, because apostolic witness concerning God's salvation must always be superior to the churchly tradition. The apostolic voice must sound without ceasing in the church.

According to the Evangelical conviction it can do this only when the Bible's mighty witness makes itself heard

in the church. Christianity does not become a kind of a
book-religion in this way, because it is not a "book" as such
which the church submits itself to but *this* Book, the one
which bears witness to God's great deeds, the Bible as
instrument for the Word of God. Evangelical thought
knows that the church lives in tradition. But it says that
Christ is the Lord of the tradition when the apostolic
message is heard, believed, and obeyed. "Those who hear
you, hear me," says Jesus. That is true according to the
Evangelical understanding in a completely literal sense.
And we hear them by simply hearing those words as they
sounded in the primitive church, both when they repeat
the words of Jesus and the events of his life and when they
proclaim Jesus as the crucified, risen, and ascended Lord
who has the entire creation in his dominion, and in whose
name alone there is salvation. This message must constantly sound in the church and in its tradition without
subtraction and without addition.

The Evangelical view calls for a strong distinction between the foundation and the building, between the basis
and that which follows, between being an apostle and not
being an apostle. The revelation as it is witnessed to in
the New Testament is not an "embryo" which will mature
in succeeding ages by the strength of a dynamic consciousness of faith in the church. The revelation is not a power
of life driving forward through the centuries which shall
bring into the light of the day what was at the beginning
only latently present. According to the Evangelical view,
we are concerned with the proclamation of a gospel which
does not need further development, which is not merely
a seed that is to grow up to be a great tree. On the
contrary, the church never tires of or stops receiving all

its nourishment from that first message of Christ as the
revelation of God who is the Lord and Savior of all the
earth. Christianity is not revelation of truth which constantly strives forward, steadily growing and becoming
richer, and discovering and exploiting new insights as a
consequence of the creative consciousness of faith.

This does not mean that Christianity is a static entity
which appears to every age in one and the same garb so
that each age has only to recover once more a completed
system of biblical truths. That would undeniably be a
misunderstanding for then one would completely overlook
the fact that the center of the biblical witness is a living
and acting God, creator and giver of life, revealed in Jesus
Christ, Lord and Savior, presently near in the Spirit, who
constantly leads the way to renewed hearing and appropriation, to faith and obedience. Down through the ages
there is constantly a new appropriation which is ever
creating new forms and methods of expression. It is, after
all, not some religious wisdom that is delivered, but a
gospel whose effective power is the risen Lord himself.
When Evangelical Christianity therefore says that tradition
is subordinate to scripture, it does not refer to a legalistic
literalism wherein the Bible is somehow considered as a
heaven-descended Koran. It means only that the biblical
witness allows its voice to be heard down through all
tradition in the midst of and, when it is demanded, *against*
our tradition. For this is a peculiarity of the Bible. It has
its voice, a voice with a peculiar independence, superiority,
and sovereignty. In the fact that the church acknowledges
the Bible's superiority to tradition, it acknowledges this
Bible's independence and freedom as it has it in itself.
The whole question of the Bible's infallibility and inspira-

tion must be seen in close relationship with its sovereignty and freedom. The fact that it constantly asserts itself in the midst of and often against our traditions is the mark of its guardianship in the church. In this manner, scripture becomes a servant of the right and true tradition, of the constantly renewed reception and spread of the gospel of God's truth and grace.

This guardianship is often thwarted by men and their traditions which have altogether too often bound and enchained the freedom and sovereignty of the Bible, whether with chains of infallible doctrine or in one or another Protestant tradition—in either orthodox or modern clothing.

The tradition may never become the "maker of its own laws." It may never, so to speak, be judge of its own case. For this reason it is not possible from the Evangelical point of view to compare the tradition with a stream, or to speak of a creative "faith-instinct" or of the so-called forward-driving powers of life that in the course of time develop the content of the faith to greater fulness and richness. There is a danger in this line of thinking of deviation or deflection away from the true tradition to a tradition which is "content with itself" and is involved in a conversation only with itself. Tradition must have, and actually does have, an absolutely superior movement over it that prevents it from becoming a self-development—no matter how religious and pious this may be. It is from this point of view that Evangelical Lutheran Christianity gives to the Bible an unqualifiedly superior place in the tradition. To say it another way, in the midst of its own tradition, constant in faith and obedience, the Evangelical church places itself under the prophetic and apostolic tradition as this is

witnessed to in the speech of the Bible and the words of
the creed.

The Evangelical church will always be sensitive to the
various voices in the church—of both "brothers and fore-
fathers." Therefore it immerses itself in the tradition of
the church with joy, and not least of all into the Roman
tradition. And it knows that it is greatly indebted to this.
It also knows that under certain circumstances, it must
allow itself to be corrected and guided by this. It must
also be willing to allow the Roman church and its tradition
to pose its very serious questions which may lead it into
very serious considerations and self-critical examinations.
A Lutheran church which is not of a mind to do this only
indicates that it has stagnated in its own tradition. But
this does not exclude for one moment that all which it
hears and learns in this manner must finally be judged by
the prophetic-apostolic voice which always asserts itself
in its freedom and sovereignty over all tradition.

In the final analysis this only means that it is the living
Lord himself in his creative and lifegiving spirit who rules
and is master over the tradition. It means that the church
must pray without ceasing: *Veni, Creator Spiritus,* "come
God, creative Spirit." Christ is the Lord of tradition. Roman
Catholic and Evangelical Lutheran Christianity may be
agreed about this. But they are not agreed about what it
means. That is, they are not agreed upon how the promise
of Christ to be with his church always until the end of the
world is being fulfilled. The Roman church sees this
promise fulfilled in the establishment of the one, defined,
and visible Roman church which alone has received the
entire truth, and the constantly richer unfolding of this
truth. Its tradition has from the beginning received a

promise of infallibility, so that the most unshakable part of the faith becomes this premise: The church and its tradition are truth.

The Evangelical church also takes this promise seriously, believing that the living Lord himself takes up his sovereign rule in the midst of the tradition of the church by constantly coming anew to his people in the living word that judges and burns, but also comforts and uplifts. The truth is not a possession but a living power which establishes its dominion. But this word of truth is intimately related to the original message about Christ as that was heard in the proclamation of the apostles and as scripture and the creed also testify. It is an Evangelical conviction that this word carries authority and responsibility in itself. And the church can judge all other tradition that appears in its life with no other measure than the apostolic word. There can never arise in the church another factor which has a similar authority. To establish another authority beside this or as an extension of this is not possible.

The authority of the church consists of constantly making relevant the biblical witness to Christ by rejecting all tradition that may later arise with claims of divine validity but which cannot establish itself legitimately as part of the original witness. A later tradition that does not conflict with the scripture and its witness is placed under the freedom of faith, but it can never be considered a truth necessary for salvation.

When this is said, it should be observed again that herewith both the Roman and every form of the Protestant tradition is placed under the same critical question. Every criticism is also a self-criticism.

Why does the Evangelical church take such a stand? Is

it a rather untimely rebelliousness? Is it the consequence of a sinful tendency to refuse to subordinate oneself to an earthly, concrete, human authority? A number of things could probably be said about this, but when all these are said something remains that does not allow itself to be categorized in this manner. The protest of the Reformers against the Roman Catholic principle of tradition and conception of authority is based upon an understanding of obedience toward the word of God which, according to their conviction, had become obscured and even set aside in the Roman church. Obedience toward God himself can never be equated with obedience toward an earthly authority—no matter how religious.

Obedience must be directed toward that God who comes to meet us in his revelation, as this is testified to in the prophetic and apostolic word of the Old and New Testaments. There is something in this witness that leads us to an understanding of tradition other than that of the Roman Catholic. This does not depend upon specific passages of scripture but upon the whole view of that remarkable phenomenon which the Bible is.

This obedience also relates to the tradition, to the religious development, and to the faith of the people, which through the changing times takes new forms. In brief, it creates tradition. The God of the Bible is not to be identified with the religious traditions of his people. He is the sovereign Lord of the tradition. The tradition has always a tendency "to run off on its own tangent," to "make deviation." Then God himself steps into his people's tradition, speaks his word, and turns the people back to himself. God must often disturb that tradition, preventing it from becoming self-sufficient, subject only to the people's religious self-development. In God's action toward his people, there is always a clear "over" and "under." This "over" is always in the final instance God himself through his sovereign action toward his people, and in his servants' sovereign, prophetic word. In this manner, <u>God in Jesus Christ had to break decisively the tradition of his people, so decisively that the people rejected his revelation and crucified Christ.</u> Christ broke the tradition and died as a sacrifice to the power of the tradition. The religious leaders of the people misunderstood the true tradition and substituted their own in its place. Christ stood within God's true tradition with his people—the tradition from Abraham, Isaac and Jacob—the tradition down through the entire history of the people, in which God alone was the acting subject.

This history repeats itself also down through the history of the new people. The struggle is between the true and genuine tradition and that tradition which constantly "runs off on its own tangent" and "makes deviation." <u>Christ alone is the Lord of the tradition</u> and the church is concerned, in the midst of its tradition, in hearing, receiving, and spreading abroad that word which has him alone as its center.

The struggle for the true understanding of the problem of scripture and tradition does not concern theological hairsplitting, but the matter itself. In this struggle Catholic and Evangelical Christians are bound together in a common "yes," and separated by a mutual "no." But above their reciprocal "yes" and "no" stands the living Lord himself, who in the midst of his church's unity and disunity will continue to fulfil his work in his creation.

Chapter 4

THE CHURCH

In the previous section we often met the word "church," a concept that has been very controversial since the time of the Reformation. It is closely connected with the problem of scripture and tradition. What was true then is also true now: in the question of the church the threads are gathered together but here the ways also separate. It is therefore necessary to investigate further what the word "church" contains according to Roman Catholic and Evangelical Lutheran insights.

Here also there is a common point of departure about which it is important to be clear. Both parties begin with the fact that there really is a church on earth and both proclaim their belief in "one, holy, Christian (Catholic) and Apostolic Church," as it is called in the Nicene Creed. This belief in the church is again built upon belief in Jesus Christ as the Son of God, Lord and Savior.

Where Jesus is only the great man, the religious genius, the exalted moral prototype, the great proclaimer, there can be no genuine understanding of the meaning of church. There Jesus may have made a mighty impact and influenced a great portion of humanity, and perhaps through his efforts may even have changed the whole course of history. Jesus has actually accomplished all this, but that

77

does not plumb the depths of the secret of his nature. Jesus has not only done his work in history as the one great outstanding personality. An association of men who hail Jesus as the great model, as the religious genius, or as the great artist of life, would not be a church or a congregation in the understanding of either the Romans or the Reformers. The church in its basic meaning exists only in that moment when there is belief in Jesus as Lord and Savior, as the crucified, risen, and ascended one, whose mission as Lord and Savior is to be continued down through all times, who in his Spirit will constantly be present with his saving power through word and sacrament. The church is not a collection of people who have come together because in one way or another they have had similar religious experiences and have the same religious opinions. The church is the new people which God himself gathers and which shall reach out to all the nations. The church is not a clique of religious people, but the church is really catholic; that is, it is appointed for all mankind, as truly as God desires to complete his salvatory work throughout his entire creation.

Both Roman and Evangelical Christianity maintain as a completely irrelinquishible fact that the church is in existence because Jesus Christ is truly the Lord and Savior of creation who, living and present, through all ages, establishes his dominion on earth. God does not desire that a certain number of individuals shall be saved out of this evil world. No, God wills a *people* of men, a new humanity, through which he will lead his work to its completion. Concerning this, Roman and Evangelical Christians are agreed. But the disagreement also begins here. Let us, as in the previous section, begin by describing the Roman view of the matter.

The first, although not the most genuine impression of the Roman church, is that of a mighty institution or organization, a visible entity with a finality and a unity, with a discipline which is at the same time pliable and movable but also severe and relentless. Roman Catholics look to this institution in obedience, honor, and love; others look at it in amazement and curiosity; still others look to it in hatred and loathing.

The institution or organization places the greatest emphasis upon the fact that it actually is a perfect earthly society, equipped with judicial and social authority, independent of any earthly state. It is a legal society with an established rule and definite ordinances which embrace all its various manifest forms and which permeate its life to the smallest details. These rules of law are collected in the so-called *Codex juris canonici*, the canonical rule lawbook with its 2414 different sections, embracing all aspects of the church's life. The church is as visible and tangible as the Kingdom of Gaul and the Republic of Venice, according to one of the great theologians of the Roman church. It can always be recognized, and very clearly be known.

Even if there be an abyss between Romanism in the various parts of the world—think for example of the difference between a primitive, superstitious, and externalized Romanism as we find it many places in South America and that sophisticated Romanism which we meet in many places in Europe—there is still the same external unity of organization, doctrine, and cultus. There is the same priesthood with the same powers, the same episcopacy with the same apostolic authority, the same mass, to a great extent the same language in the mass and other worship, and the same faith with the same dogmas. No matter how different the setting of these things may be—and that difference may often be so great that one wonders if they are really concerned about the same things—there is nevertheless a powerful unity.

And that unity has its strongest expression in the submission to the Roman bishop, the pope. In the final analysis obedience to the pope is the decisive recognizable sign of whether one is or is not a Roman Catholic. Even if one accepts the entire body of Catholic belief, if one does not acknowledge the pope, one is nevertheless not a Roman Catholic Christian. Without relationship to the successor of Peter in the Holy See there does not exist any genuine Christianity and there is no church. And turn it about: where the pope is, there is Christ's true and only church. He is the one and the supreme shepherd over the flock of Christ. "To be a Catholic—not only in name but also in fact—there is only one means, one alone, but this in turn is indispensable and irreparable: to obey the Church and its superior, to think as the Church and its superior." Pope Pius XI wrote in 1931 in this manner to Cardinal Schuster in Milan with respect to fascism. It is therefore necessary for us to consider for a moment the question of the pope as the successor of Peter and viceroy of Christ on earth.

A). b. The official title of the pope is: "His Holiness the Pope, Bishop of Rome, Vicar of Jesus Christ on Earth, Successor of Peter the Prince of the Apostles, Supreme Pontiff of the Universal Church, Patriarch of the West, Primate of Italy, Archbishop and Metropolitan of the Roman Church

Province, and Sovereign of the Temporal Dominion of the
Holy Roman Church."

When the Roman pope is legally elected and has accepted the election, he occupies with divine right the full
authority of the supreme rule. No decision of any council
has any binding power unless it is confirmed by the pope
and proclaimed on his command. A matter that the pope
has decided cannot be appealed to a general council. If it
should happen that the pope should die during the meeting
of a general council, the meeting or council must then be
interrupted until a new pope has been elected and has
decided that the meeting may be taken up again and
continued. The pope has the highest and most unlimited
authority in the church, and all within the church owe to
him unconditional obedience, not only in matters of faith
and moral questions, but in every thing that belongs to the
discipline and order of the church throughout the entire
world. The pope not only shares in the authority of the
church but possesses it in its completeness; actually, he is
that authority himself. He has not received this authority
from the church—neither from a council nor from the other
bishops. He has his authority solely and directly from God.
His office is not conditional upon his own person or the
character of his own life. No matter who he is—even if he
should be an immoral person—he possesses this absolute
authority in which he is absolutely and completely independent of every earthly power. "Rome has spoken; the
matter is decided."

It is this authority in matters of faith and morals which
was established as dogma by the Vatican council in Rome
in 1870. This decision reads:

We teach and define that it is a dogma divinely revealed, that the Roman Pontiff, when he speaks _ex cathedra_, that is; when, in discharge of the office of pastor and doctor of all Christians, by virtue of his supreme Apostolic authority, he defines a doctrine regarding faith or morals to be held by the Universal Church, by the divine assistance promised to him in blessed Peter, is possessed of that infallibility with which the divine Redeemer willed that his Church should be endowed for defining doctrine regarding faith or morals; and that, therefore, such definitions of the Roman Pontiff are irreformable of themselves and not from the consent of the Church.

When we evaluate this statement and try to clarify what it really contains, we must ask: What is it that causes Roman Catholicism to have bestowed upon an individual person such unlimited power and authority in the church? The Roman church justifies the bestowal of this power by referring to the position of leadership that Jesus gave to Peter among the apostles. This turns upon the famous passage in the Gospel according to Matthew (Matt. 16: 18-19).

Here Jesus gave to Peter the all-embracing power and authority to rule and judge, absolute infallibility in matters of faith; in short the role of the rock in the church, without which there neither is nor can be a church. Furthermore this was not given to Peter alone but to all his successors as well. To be sure this cannot be concluded from this biblical passage where there is no reference to anyone besides Peter, but without this understanding the text is meaningless according to the Roman reading. Later history has, after all, shown that this was the intent. Peter went to Rome and died there as the bishop, and the promise given to him is valid also to all his successors as bishops of Rome. As it is the will of God that Peter as the foremost of the apostles should have successors and as these successors of Peter obviously are the bishops of Rome, the words of Jesus to Peter also pertain with divine significance to all the bishops of Rome, all the succeeding popes.

It is not dogmatically defined but it is the common opinion of Roman theologians that it was the will of Christ that the bishops of Rome specifically should assume Peter's position in the church, and that this was most likely also indicated to Peter by Christ himself. After the ascension of Christ, the church is not built upon Christ alone but also upon Peter who is the visible foundation of the church. Christ and his viceroy are only one head for the church. For this reason Pope Pius XII writes in his encyclical concerning the church that those who maintain that they can worship Christ as the head of the church without acknowledging Peter as the representative of Christ find themselves in a dangerous error. It is true that Christ is the church's only Lord who has the inner invisible leadership, but Christ does not rule his church in an invisible manner, and it is through his representative on earth that he exercises a visible and divinely-instituted leadership of his mystical body. For this reason salvation is closely connected with submission to this representative.

As will be seen, there is a very close relationship between this view and the concept of tradition as we described it in the previous chapter. It can very briefly be stated in this manner: in the last analysis the pope himself represents the tradition. It is said that Pope Pius IX, who was pope at the time when the infallibility of the pope was established by the church meeting in Rome in 1870, was informed that this doctrine concerning the papacy did not have the complete support of the tradition. He is supposed to have replied: "The tradition? I am the tradition."

Whether or not this is historically true, it does cover the matter. To be sure the Pope has spoken *ex cathedra* only once since that council, that is as the infallible teacher of the church, namely at the proclamation of the last Mary dogma in November, 1950. But his unique position naturally gives all his words a very significant weight and his various encyclicals also have a particularly binding power.

This power naturally reaches out first and foremost over all who are within the Roman church, but it is actually valid for all who are baptized. Also those who are baptized outside the Roman church—if the baptism is rightly administered—belong to the pope and are subject to his authority. This received a clear expression when Pope Pius IX wrote to Kaiser Wilhelm I during the *Kulturkampf* and said: "I speak in order to fulfil one of my duties which consists of speaking the truth to all, also to those who are not Catholics. For everyone who has been baptized belongs in one way or another to the Pope, which matter cannot be explained further here."

We are also told hereby how the Roman church must view other church groups. This may briefly be stated that in the eyes of God there actually does not exist any church other than the Roman Catholic. No other church can claim the name of church; all others must be considered sects.

The Roman church's view of itself has had a famous expression in the well-known sentence: "Extra ecclesiam nulla salus," ("Outside the church there is no salvation"), a sentence that has been extraordinarily discussed both outside and within the Roman church. The sentence probably originates with Cyprian, but received its sharpest elaboration in the famous bull of Boniface VIII in 1302, which reads: "We declare and decide that it is necessary for the salvation of every human that he submit himself to the Roman Pope." One of the most incisive expressions in more recent times comes from Pope Pius IX who said, "It is a pernicious error which has crept into many Catholic hearts, that one may look with assurance upon all those who do not belong to the Catholic Church. It must be maintained on the contrary as a dogma that no one can be saved outside the apostolic Roman Church and that it is the only Ark of salvation so that he who does not enter therein will perish in the great Flood." In 1864 the Pope expressed himself further that "the belief which says that someone may hope for the salvation of those who are not to be found within the true Church of Christ ought to be condemned." These would seem to be clear enough expressions that would justify those who say that according to the Roman Catholic point of view all those are lost who do not belong to the external visible church.

Actually this is not right. Directly following the first cited expression of Pope Pius IX, he adds, "Nevertheless it ought just as surely to be maintained that they who live in ignorance of the true religion—if this ignorance is insurmountable—are not guilty in the eyes of God." Recently in America some priests maintained that there was no salvation outside of the visible Roman church. They were emphatically disavowed by Rome which took the occasion to refresh again the Catholic teaching on this point. On the one hand it was firmly maintained that there is no salvation outside the Roman Catholic church. Only there can be found the means of grace necessary for salvation. However it is possible to belong to the Roman church without finding oneself within the jurisdiction of the church in externals. There can exist a longing even if completely unconscious within a person to belong to the church and that is sufficient if not *in re,* i.e., in external reality, then nevertheless *in voto,* i.e., according to desire and longing to belong to the Roman Catholic church. "The Body of Christ transcends in its mystical reality the limits of the visible, organized Church," says Dominican Father Lutz in Oslo.

Those men from other church communions, or even the heathens who have no relationship with any form of Christianity, who are in good faith and by no fault of their own are in ignorance of the true faith, belong to the church by virtue of their faithfulness toward those truths which they have recognized and their innermost unconscious desire, and are therefore not without salvation. In his encyclical of 1943, Pope Pius XII cautiously states that those who do not belong to the visible fellowship of the Roman church find themselves in a situation in which they cannot be certain of their salvation. "For even if they as a consequence of an unconscious longing and desire already stand in a relationship to the Redeemer's mystical body, nevertheless they do need so many efficacious divine gifts of grace and helping means, which one can only derive benefit from as a member of the Catholic Church."

The sentence, "Outside the church there is no salvation," is thus a sentence which can be interpreted in both a broader and a narrower sense. The official position of the Roman church purports to present that sentence in its strength; but by allowing the distinction of belonging in the external, visible manner or belonging in accord with one's innermost desire, it tends to mitigate the strict interpretation. This broader interpretation is perhaps partly related to the fact that the sharper attitude toward Protestants, which were earlier spoken of as rebels and as a people who had made their belly their god, has softened and has been replaced by a more conciliatory tone. Evangelical Christians are now often spoken of as "our separated brothers" or "our Protestant brothers." A similar development has also taken place within the Evangelical church.

If such a rather far-reaching tolerance does exist for those who guiltlessly do not belong to the visible Catholic church, there is in contrast a great rigidity toward those who stand within the church. No valid ground can ever be given for doubting the Roman church and its truth, at any rate not among Catholics who have received the proper education in the truths of the faith. If someone should fall into doubt, there must be moral defects that are to blame. To give up the Catholic faith and step over into another Christian fellowship cannot be morally justified. Coercive measures toward persons are justified in case of defection or heresy. Religious freedom as such is not a good thing, and it is not good when a Catholic state relinquishes the unity of faith. One nation, one religion.

Have we then with all this sufficiently described the Roman conception of the church? Actually, no, for we have so far only considered one side of the matter. We have viewed the church as an external, legal institution, as a monarchical state with the pope at its head and with bishops as shepherds and superintendents with apostolic authority, who have been established as successors of the apostles by the Holy Spirit. We have as yet only been occupied with the external aspects of the church which after all is only one side of the picture. Protestants are often tempted to stop here and allow their judgment to fall on the basis of that which has thus far been presented.

We can get an interesting insight into the Roman concept of the church by taking a look at church history. (The following has been borrowed from a Roman theologian.)

The various epochs of history have developed different sides to the character of the Roman Catholic church. One can very well speak of transformations or changes in the concept of the church as conditioned by historical circumstances, if one is sure to make it clear that this does not mean real change, but a development in which that which previously existed preserves its truth.

In the early church, the church was the new people of God who were rescued out of this evil world and who awaited the second coming of the Lord in the very near future. It did not recognize any responsibility to permeate society but rather sought to remain outside of the worldly life as much as possible. Everything was still in many ways completely undeveloped. The Roman bishop had not yet asserted his absolute lordship in the church. There were bishops who denied that there resided any particular authority in the bishop of Rome. The Christians knew themselves as the body of Christ, as his bride, as a people that belonged to him and whose head was the risen Christ himself. The various organs of the body were the functional servants necessary for the edification of the body and its fulfilment. Separation from the world had as its counterpart a fervent brotherly love. Christians were hated for the most part by the contemporary heathen world and were more inclined toward the coming than the present world.

But the Lord did not come. Consequently the barriers against the world fell. After the "liberating deed" of Emperor Constantine made Christianity into the religion of the state, Christians were forced to turn toward the world and to seek to permeate the worldly orders with Christian ideas. Later, in the midst of the collapse of Rome, the church showed itself to be the rescuing power and at the same time became the educator of the young Germanic peoples. In brief, the church began to show itself in all its secular power.

This conception of the church received historical-philosophical elaboration in the grandiose view of Augustine: The church as God's state on earth. Here begins the dream of the Middle Ages: the church as the visible kingdom of God here on earth, anchored in agreement between the spiritual and secular rulers and in which all human activity and all worldly conditions were to be formed and influenced by the Christian faith and submissive to divine law. The Roman bishop stands at the head of this City of God. He has the supreme power and possesses both the secular and the spiritual sword.

Outwardly, the church of the Middle Ages was the great power church, to which the powers of this world were forced to submit. To a great extent, the pope and the bishops entered into political activity and themselves became powers in the world. This universal, creative and powerful concept of the church had its own legitimacy but also its obvious dangers. For this reason the church had to develop further in order to give expression to other sides of the nature of the church. Not that the view of the Middle Ages is to be forgotten. On the contrary, it constantly stands as an essential link in the Roman understanding of the church. Among other things, it lies behind the phenomenon that we know today as "political Catholicism."

With the close of the Middle Ages, the Roman church entered upon a new phase which again changed the face of the church.

Now the Roman church was no longer the only church but was surrounded by churches who also made claims to be the church of Jesus Christ. In many ways the Roman church was under indictment and forced to battle for its very existence. This struggle in which it constantly claimed to be the only saving church in contrast to all the "sham churches" gave to it a narrow, often arrogant, and unsympathetic stamp that caused the opposition and distrust of the non-Roman Christian. The proud church of the Middle Ages became—to put it sharply—"The church of the ghetto." It became a church whose legalistic nature was emphasized; the anti-Protestant polemic became characteristic of the face of the church. The church of modern times became to a greater and greater degree a church of authority, a church of dogma, wherein the pope time after time was called upon to condemn and to instruct.

In this period when the church had to appear again and again as the instructor and disciplinarian, the church's own children inevitably came to feel themselves restrained. There rose a rift between the lay people and the hierarchy of the church, who alone had the rule. This resulted in the word "church" bringing to the minds of most Catholics a concept of authority and power, and they themselves no longer experienced being a church. When catechisms came to the explanation of the church, they presented it in terms of judicial power and infallible doctrine.

The church in this period, from the Council of Trent to the present day, may therefore be seen essentially as the church of the pope with a strong, centralized rule. Never before has the pope had such great significance and influence. This received its clearest expression at the Vatican Council of 1870 when the dogma of papal infallibility was adopted.

Nevertheless this development was not without its drawbacks. It was accompanied by an incapacitation and crippling of laymen, and even of the bishops and priests. Much initiative was smothered and the distance between the church and the world grew steadily larger.

A peculiar feature of our time is that this concept of the church is also going into the melting pot. The development we are witnessing in our day is of a double nature. In part, there is a trend toward amazing independence on the part of the lay people, to a renewal of the idea of the common priesthood of the baptized, a ferment which is still in its nascent state. Everyone who knows a little bit about what the phrase "Catholic Action" contains, understands something of what is taking place here. In part, there is a trend toward a new understanding of the inner mystical nature of the church that focuses itself upon the church as the "body of Christ." In this there is a return to the New Testament and apostolic concept of the church and often a rather strong criticism of the view of the church of earlier times.

It is noteworthy that in the midst of World War II, Pope Pius XII found reason to send out an encyclical with the title: *Mystici Corporis Christi* ("Concerning the Mystical Body of Christ," June 29, 1943). Now the Pope sought to define the nature of the church clearly and plainly by returning to a biblical concept. What is the principal point of this papal encyclical? Of course, the Roman church is upheld as the only legal and true church, where the pope as the viceroy of Christ has final authority; and the pope takes the occasion seriously to warn those who in blind, reformatory zeal overstep the boundaries of a sound understanding of this point. But the main concern is nevertheless the description of the church as a spiritual organism, wherein Christ in a mystical manner works incessantly, infusing his sanctifying grace into the individual members through the sacraments. Jesus Christ contains all supernatural gifts in all their abundance and perfection. By way of the church and its means of grace these stream from him to mankind and sanctify mankind. Even as the church could never exist without its head, neither could Christ exist without his body. The body can actually be called the consummation and completeness of Christ.

The church has its external aspects—all the functions through which the truth is proclaimed and grace conferred. This may be called the bodily aspect of the church. But just as the humanity of Christ was a means of his divine nature, so is the church's external body of outer things, functions, and persons an instrument through which the divine life is transmitted to men. The church's bodily aspect is the continuation of the human nature of Christ. The church is the second Christ, the Christ himself who continues his life here on earth, mystically bound to his body through the holy functions of the church executed by those persons consecrated for that purpose. We have herewith reached the final stratum of the Roman understanding of the church: the church as the mystical body of Christ, as the supernatural and sacramental organism of salvation in which Christ is intimately and inseparably bound to his faithful and they to him.

In the following account of the Evangelical view of the

church, it must first of all be noted that we are emerging from a period of the history of the Evangelical church in which there has been a very weak consciousness of what it is to be a church. Of course, this has not been true everywhere, but it is nevertheless true to a considerable degree as we consider Protestantism in its entirety. About the turn of the century, Adolf V. Harnack, who was probably the most significant Protestant historian and theologian at that time, gave a series of lectures at the University of Berlin concerning "What Is Christianity?" In these lectures he described what Christianity was without seriously entering into the concept of the church. The theme was that Christianity was chiefly to be regarded, as an individualistic relationship to God. The church had significance only of second or third rank and did not belong to that which was essential.

The famous theologian, Wilhelm Hermann, at one time visited the University at Uppsala. Here he met the man later to become so well known as professor and bishop, Gustaf Aulén, who at this very time was working on his disputation on Luther's conception of the church. When Hermann heard of this, he is reported to have said: "I congratulate Swedish theology that it has so much time and peace that it can occupy itself with something so peripheral." This view made itself felt far beyond theological circles.

Many Evangelical Christians would have been lost for an answer had they been asked what the church really was or what it meant to them. There may be various appraisals of this, as there are various views of these matters, but there can hardly be any doubt that this attitude toward the church was a fruit—many will add, a bitter fruit—of the age of enlightenment with its individualism, and its tendency to change and dissolve the biblical, reformation understanding of Christianity.

In the meantime a great change has taken place on this very point in our time. The question of the church has again become living and actual. In part, exegetical research has led to a renewed understanding of the significance of the church in the primitive church as we find it in the New Testament; and in part, the times themselves have led to renewed questions concerning the church and the fellowship of the church. A Roman theologian wrote some years ago, "He who today asks about Christianity, is asking about the church." This is also true to a large extent in the Evangelical camp. "To have a church, a mother, which from youth could lead my steps, became the thirst and longing of my life," said the Dutch statesman and theologian, Abraham Kuyper.

It has been said in the meantime from the Roman side that the viewpoint of the Reformers was that God spoke his word to the individual man in some mystical manner that was completely independent of external means and independent of any community with other men. The Reformers were said to be basically consistent individualists. This is completely incorrect. For the Reformers also, God has related his word to a church, a community of men, to very definite, external words, to specific deeds. The fellowship of the church and its "signs," both the preaching of the word and the administration of the sacraments, precede the faith of the individual and are the means through which God encounters the individual. Modern individualism with its contempt for externals and its lack of understanding of community with others and therewith of the essential content of the word "church" does not stem from the Reformers but has other roots. The church is not for the Reformers any more than for the Roman Catholics something incidental, minor, and unessential. It is rather something basic, not only as a means, but something that indissolubly belongs to God's work of salvation.

For this reason Luther calls the church our "mother," which gives us birth and nurtures us, without which we could not even become Christians and come to Christ as our Lord and Savior. And it was Calvin who gave expression to these beautiful words, "We may learn from the title of *mother*, how useful and even necessary it is for us to know her; since there is no other way of entrance into life, unless we are conceived by her, born of her, nourished at her breast, and continually preserved under her care and government till we are divested of this mortal flesh and become like the angels. For our frailty does not allow us to depart from this school but in our entire life we must be its disciple. Even more: outside of her lap there can be no hope for the remission of sins."

When the Reformers felt themselves compelled to leave the great church, it was not in any case because they denied or were indifferent toward the fact of the church. The question debated by Roman and Evangelical Christians is not whether or not there shall be a church but what this church is. Because the question of the true church occupied the Reformers both day and night they finally came to a break with the mighty Roman church. It was not because the Reformers were rebels who wished to split and divide at any price. Just the opposite. It was rather because, compelled in their conscience, they desired to be servants of the true church. They knew that it is not possible for men to present themselves before God as the pure church, but rather it is God who in his loving kindness constantly renews his church. That is, it was not they who were to build the new church. The church had always been. But they knew themselves compelled to place themselves at the disposal of that renewal which they saw to be necessary.

It will be necessary as a beginning to consider the Evangelical interpretation of that important passage in the Gospel according to Matthew (Matt. 16:18) on which the Roman church bases its view of the church: "And I tell you, you are Peter, and on this rock I will build my church, and the powers of death shall not prevail against it."

The disagreement concerning the meaning of this passage did not arise either yesterday or the day before, but has existed since at least the beginning of the third century. In the first two centuries we find only vague reference to the passage in Christian literature—actually it was not cited in its entirety during this period—and the church fathers who do treat the passage understand it in very divergent ways. Tertullian regards this word as one that pertains to Peter only and dissociates himself from the view that it is relevant to the bishops of Rome. Cyprian thinks of it as relevant to all bishops. Peter is on the same plane in his office and his authority as the other bishops and has no rank superior to theirs. Peter is always the sign of the unity of the church, but it is the bishops in their entirety who constitute that unity.

Origen stands quite alone in his interpretation. He spiritualizes the entire passage and finds in the person of Peter not only the apostle but "every Peter"—i.e., that this is true of all believing and confessing followers of Christ.

Origen rejects the thought that the church shall be built solely and only on Peter, as Peter has no precedence over all the others who believe and confess. The passage thus speaks of all believers.

Eusebius of Caesarea interprets Christ to be the rock and in a wider sense sees Peter as the rock, the one who confesses that Jesus is the Christ, Son of the living God. Chrysostom says of this passage, "You are Christ, and on this rock I will build my Church, that is to say: on that faith which you have confessed." But because Peter is the first of all the disciples to make this confession and is for that reason the first to go into the church, he does deserve a certain place of honor. He became the most prominent apostle and the founder of the church.

Nor does the Western church of the first three centuries have a unanimous interpretation of the passage. Bishop Ambrose of Milan does not speak of Peter as the foundation of the church. He strongly underscores the significance of Peter's faith, and it is as a man of faith that he has greater authority for teaching than the other apostles. It is in this respect, and not as one who governs and is given jurisdiction, that Rome has inherited Peter's charge.

It is naturally important to observe what Augustine found in the passage. He knew that its interpretation was difficult and had two understandings of it himself. For some it was Peter who was the rock, for others, Christ; and it was this last conception toward which Augustine leaned. "For it does not say: You are *the rock,* but you are Peter. The rock was Christ whom Peter confessed—as the entire church also confesses him—and by whom he was called Peter." It was Peter who received his name from the rock and not the rock which receives its name from Peter.

When Jesus said that "upon this rock I will build my church," it means "upon that rock on which Peter has just confessed his faith." Peter himself is built upon that rock. But at the same time Peter is the living symbol, the archetype of the entire church.

Augustine knew that the choice could be difficult enough to make and allowed the reader himself to determine which of the two interpretations was correct. He did not give an authoritative explanation. However Augustine's vacillation on this did not hinder him from assigning a precedence to Peter even as the Roman bishopric was also given a rank above the others.

Later in the fifth century, however, the matter became much clearer for the Western church. At any rate since Leo I (d. 461) this Matthean passage was considered, as a matter of course, to concern in part Peter and in part his successors upon the bishop's seat in Rome. In the meantime the Eastern church went its own way, and the Greek Orthodox church today does not recognize the primacy of Peter to be valid for the Roman bishops. The rock is understood to be Christ himself; or it is the faith of Peter in Christ. Where Peter is regarded as the rock, he has only a limited personal precedence as the most prominent apostle.

These broad references are sufficient to indicate that there is by no means unanimity with respect to the understanding of this passage from Matthew. On the contrary, divergent interpretations have existed ever since the early church. The Reformers are not simply telling fairy tales in their exposition of the passage but have many predecessors in the ancient church.

Luther regards the rock as Christ. This rock is the Son of God, Jesus Christ alone, and none other. You are the

Discussion of the Rock.

man of the rock, Jesus says to Peter, for you have confessed
and proclaimed the true man who is the true rock such as
the Scriptures designate him, namely Christ. Peter is the
rock because he stands upon the rock and thereby becomes
of rock himself. In and of himself Peter is everything but
a rock, as the immediately succeeding verses clearly show.
"Therefore Christ allowed Peter to fall, that we might not
regard him as the rock and build upon him. For we must
have our foundation upon him who can stand against all
devils, and that is Christ."

Calvin says that this passage deals with Peter's faith in
Christ. The faith which confesses that Jesus is the Christ—
which confesses together with and according to the example
of the apostle Peter—is the rock on which the church is
to be built.

A unique and interesting solution is proposed by a scholar
who translates the text back into Aramaic, the mother
tongue of Jesus, and thereby arrives at the following text:
"I say unto you, yes, you, Peter, that upon this rock
(namely Christ, the Son of the living God) I will build my
church." In recent Protestantism there are many who have
gone a completely different way and have declared that
the word does not originate from Christ himself but is
added later at a time and place where it was desirable to
promote the person of Peter. It is very improbable that
these words are from the mouth of Jesus. I do not intend
to enter this discussion further. It only gives one more
indication of how little certainty there is if one is to take
a stand solely and completely on historical grounds. Here
we will allow the words to stand as they are, and try to
understand them within their context.

In the following I shall briefly consider Oscar Cullmann's

book, *Peter: Disciple-Apostle-Martyr,*[1] a recent investigation of this question on Protestant grounds. It is interesting because it treats the question archeologically, exegetically, and dogmatically, and not least because Cullmann in many ways agrees with the Roman exegesis without however drawing the same conclusions. The book has attracted much attention in Roman as well as Protestant theological circles.

Even if Cullmann doubts that these words were spoken on the same occasion that Matthew's Gospel records, he is in no doubt that we do meet here a genuine word of Christ. Nor is he in doubt that the word is spoken directly to Peter and pertains to him personally. Here he accordingly diverges from the interpretation of the Reformers. The word is directed toward the *apostle* Peter and implies all that power with which an apostle is provided and which no one can later receive. We find in a unique way a foundation, a word that indicates a cornerstone. Peter is that rock upon which the entire church is later to be built. The rock lies as a foundation; it is something "once and for all," something that lies firmly and plays a role that cannot be transfered to anything else. Those who followed after could be and were exceedingly important: deacons, presbyters, bishops, prophets, teachers, and shepherds; but they were certainly not the foundation, not apostles, who filled a very special place as the ones personally chosen by Christ. It was exactly those who took this word unto themselves who were unfaithful to that to which they were called, namely to build upon the only foundation that existed. At this moment this was Peter, the confessing one, the apostle, the

[1] Translated from the German by Floyd V. Filson (Philadelphia: Westminster Press, 1953).

chosen one. All those who followed had only to see that the
foundation, the rock, lay secure and immovable there
where Christ had laid it.

We note how the whole question of scripture and tradition discussed in the previous chapter also enters here. If
we are to ask how, according to this understanding, Peter
can be the basis of the church through all later ages, the
answer must be: that all subsequent church ages must
build on the basis which is Peter. That is, to be solid and
unswerving in faithfulness to his witness to Christ as it is
testified to in the creed and scripture. At that moment
Peter stood as the representative for that faith in Christ
upon which all depends. Aside from this basis there is no
rock but only sand. In this way Peter and the other
apostles bore the responsibility for building the church.

The Evangelical view, as Cullmann represents it, makes
a case for the apostolicity of the church equal to that of
the Roman church. For him, apostolicity means: built upon
Peter as the first apostle, who confessed Jesus as the Christ,
the Son of the living God; not upon a chance person or an
arbitrary observer, e.g., a Roman historian or a modern
historian of religion. It is built on that very apostle who
was a man of personal weakness—as the following account
in the Gospel according to Matthew so clearly indicates—
but who nevertheless by God's own revelation makes that
confession upon which all depends: "You are Christ, the
Son of the living God." The very cornerstone is Christ,
himself. The foundation is the apostles, because they were
chosen to be his witnesses, and upon their witness the
church was built and must be built as long as there is
a church upon the earth. The church which would continue to build, must only continue faithful to that founda-

tion, the confessing apostle and that church in which he had the leadership.

The leadership which was given to Peter and to the other apostles must also continue in the church, not in an external, mechanical manner—Christ had given no command to that effect—but in such a way that Peter becomes the original model for all leadership. The church is truly given the power to proclaim with authority, to declare the forgiveness of sins, and where man will not hear the call to repentance, to refuse it. There is a "power of the keys" in the church. Jesus gave the authority of leadership to Peter for that early period in which the foundations were laid, but did not at all imply that the same authority would belong to specific men—namely, the bishops of Rome—after the time of Peter. There is not the slightest hint of such intent in the text itself or in the oldest tradition. It is a decisive difficulty from an Evangelical point of view that there is no support in biblical texts for one of the most important of all the doctrines of the Roman Catholic church—that only that church which acknowledges the Roman bishop is the one and true church of Jesus Christ. Even if it should be the case that Peter later came to Rome and died there, which Cullmann as historian does not find sufficient evidence to deny, there is by no means sufficient ground to guarantee such an extraordinary and extensive conclusion.

To base the Roman Catholic theory of the church, with its enormously far-reaching consequences, upon a passage of scripture like this is placing altogether too great a strain upon this text, especially since the claim cannot plead the support of early tradition. The Evangelical view must say "no" to this interpretation, which on the basis of this pas-

sage makes it possible to assign such power and authority
to the bishop in Rome as no other man has ever had before
or since. This is a disastrous confusion of foundation and
structure. It is a historic fact that the Roman bishop, the
pope, has had great importance and to a degree still has it.
Evangelicals must recognize this and ascribe to that office
its proper significance. But Evangelicals cannot agree that
the Roman bishops are the fundamental basis and mainstay
of the church of Christ on earth through all ages and that
this is verified not humanly or historically, but with unqualified divine right. Here there is an "either-or."

This is arrived at on purely historical grounds as these
have been developed above. Not a few Roman theologians
do grant a measure of concession today—that to be sure
one cannot conclusively prove the position of the Roman
bishop by this passage in Matthew—but the essential fact
is that Rome with its bishops actually did, in the course
of history, receive the leadership of the church. Therefore
one may return to this text with the conclusion that even
if history is opaque, there can be no doubt that Matthew
16:18 was also relevant to the successors of Peter. This
was the will of God for his church. Otherwise God must
have provided poorly for it.

There are those Roman theologians who go a step further
and maintain that the decisive fact is not at all whether
Peter was ever in Rome or not. In the final analysis that is
more a question that belongs in the realm of faith than of
history. The fact that the Roman bishop is the successor of
Peter with all that power which was bestowed upon Peter
is of primary importance and a concept that we know to
be a major link in the Roman faith. It is something that is
to be believed by virtue of revelation.

Logically, we are confronted by a strange circular argument. the Roman bishop is the successor of Peter, and the viceroy of Christ is maintained through faith with tradition as the source of the revelation. In the light of this later tradition the passage in Matthew 16 is to be interpreted. But that tradition is a source of the revelation, should be verified by history, i.e., by the scripture passage in Matthew and by the oldest apostolic tradition.

The conclusion of these considerations must be that, in the last analysis, historical research is not the basis on which one decides whether or not to hold the Roman view. This depends upon deeper matters and other considerations. According to the Roman point of view, this question, as other questions of faith, can only be solved when divine grace intervenes and enlightens human minds.

An essential point in these considerations is certainly found in the fact that only through the Roman way of thinking can men be sure of their faith. Otherwise everything collapses. The guarantee—to use an expression which is perhaps too heavy-handed for the Roman Catholic but which I use for the sake of clarity—for the truth of Christianity can only be given through this certainty in the infallibility of the church, concentrated on the person of the pope as the successor of Peter and as the viceroy of Christ. The true apostolic witness is found *eo ipso* where the pope and the bishops are, as something given beforehand. There is the truth of Christ, and there is Christ himself. Jesus has issued, so to speak, a "blank check" to Peter which reads that wherever the Roman pope may be, there truth is to be found for all time.

It must clearly be noted that the Evangelical church does not have this guarantee. It stands far less protected, much more naked and unguaranteed. There is much less to see, much less that is tangible, without any apparent external support. It must be conceded that there is very little here to take hold of. But the strange thing is that the Evangelical view, particularly where it burst out in strength and power, always stood unguaranteed and unprotected and did not make its way because it first had proved its reasonableness or gain the religious support of man. Where the word broke through, it did not need any external support or guarantee. It was Christ himself who stood behind it.

Wherever the Evangelical view is genuine and does not succumb to the temptation to seek external guarantees and props, there is a certain distinct distrust of external supports, of a constructed, tangible system of guarantees. It is as if the word's own original power loses its authority and conviction by this strange direct identificaton of the human and the divine. Pope Pius XII wrote in an encyclical that, after the ascension of Christ, the church no longer builds upon Christ alone but also on Peter as the viceroy of Christ on earth, and that these two now constitute one head (as is also expressed by Boniface VIII, the pope who more than any other during the Middle Ages made the claim for the absolute power of the pope). Evangelicals deny that this is a true view of the lordship of Christ in the church. It was this very view that aroused the Reformers and led them to make their harsh judgment on the pope, even to make the accusation that he was the Antichrist—not of course in his person, but as representative of the institution which laid claim to divine authority.

The Evangelicals ask the mighty institution of the Roman Catholic church if the lordship of Christ is not hereby

confused with the lordship of the Roman Catholic church
and if it does not thereby identify itself with Christ and
makes itself independent in its relationship to Christ. Such
an infallible church, according to the Roman understanding, is secured by divine supports and guarantees, in which
Christ and the Holy Spirit have become one with the
immanent life of the church. As the judicial, authoritative
and supernatural church of grace it *is* the onliving Christ
and is therefore according to the Evangelical conviction,
no longer completely and essentially depending on Christ
as its only Lord. That is not to say of course that Christ
in his freedom and grace does not make himself Lord in
the Roman Catholic church. That question is not raised
here. We are concerned with the principle itself, the theological understanding of the nature of the church.

It is conceded that Romans will have a great deal of
difficulty in understanding this question, which to most of
them will certainly appear to be both awkward and unreasonable. Nevertheless the question must be asked: Has
not Christ here been identified with a definite, earthly,
human church and its power and extension? Has not Christ
here been identified with the church as a religious organization? And therefore He is no longer Lord?

Here we face the most serious and profound problem
of the church—that which spiritually sensitive readers
catch a glimpse of in a harrowing manner in Dostoevsky's
story of the Grand Inquisitor in the novel *The Brothers
Karamazov*. He who is unaffected by the indictment of this
story can hardly sense the problem of the church and its
temptation. But we must add in the same breath that this
question directs itself to both the Roman and the Evangelical church, even to every church upon the earth. Every

church meets the temptation of establishing itself as a religious bloc, perhaps provided with great worldly power and influence, as a power of social influence, as an apparatus of piety and an organ of grace, as a servant of the inner religiosity of all men.

In the midst of all this the church may be an utterly apostate church, no longer an implement for the coming of God's Kingdom or for the salvatory power of Christ, but a tool of the great apostasy, the spirit of the world. Such a church would more than gladly clothe itself in the garb of religion or, even better, in Christianity, in order all the more anonymously to fulfil the mission of apostasy among the peoples of the world. The church which does not hear this question but protects itself behind some claim of divine security, perhaps in the refuge of its own native piety and sanctity, is in danger of becoming a church of apostasy. And this is true no matter what the church is called—Roman Catholic or Evangelical Lutheran. No fine theory as such, Roman or Evangelical, can help a church here. For that reason every church must turn back to the prayer that Christ may assume sovereign lordship.

Luther energetically maintains that God's church is ruled by the Holy Spirit himself, that Christ is with his church on earth until the end of the world. For this reason we pray daily in our confession of faith: "We believe in one holy, catholic (universal) church." But Luther bases his belief in the church not upon a visible church with an infallible leadership, but upon Christ alone. Christ in his free grace will constantly come and through his word and holy sacraments establish his rule upon the earth. "Ecclesia semper reformanda est," said one of the theologians of the Reformation period. "The Church must constantly undergo

reform." This must be true without restriction for all ages.
This does not mean a reformation which is such a cease-
less merry-go-round that finally no one knows what is up
or down—that would be a shocking caricature of reformation—but a reformation in which the church always openly
listens to God's word in his revelation. That word can
never be identified with the church itself but is always
absolutely superior to the church and always battles against
the church for the church.

"It is after all not we who can uphold the church, nor
was it our predecessors, nor will it be our successors," says
Luther, "but it was, it is, and it always will be He who
says: I am with you always even to the end of the age,
Jesus Christ."

When access to a church meeting at Augsburg was
denied Luther, he wrote a letter to Melanchthon who was
representing the cause of the Evangelicals. In a moment
of discouragement, and pressed by overwhelming difficulties and great opposition, Melanchthon had expressed
a doubt in the cause of the Reformation. Luther then
wrote to him to this effect: "You say that you do not know
where it all will lead to. But I wish to say that if our cause
is dependent upon your rhetoric or upon anything else
that is human, then I will have nothing to do with bringing it about. Our cause belongs to only one thing, namely
the faith. And faith is this: to place one's cause exclusively
in God." In this faith alone that God both can and will
lead his cause to victory, that he will allow his word to
be heard—that word which has never been bound by any
human power—that he will provide for his church until
the end of time, lies the most genuine part of the Reformers'
view of the church.

At the Evangelical church meeting at Barmen, Germany, in 1934 it was necessary to take a stand on the very pressing external situation caused by Hitler's usurpation of power and the "German-Christian" movement in the church. The Lutheran and the Reformed theologians assembled there adopted the following definition of the church, based on Ephesians 4:15-16: "The Christian church is the community of brothers where Jesus Christ in word and sacrament through the Holy Spirit today acts as Lord. With its faith as well as its obedience, with its message as well as its order, in the midst of the world of sin and as the church of forgiven sinners, it shall witness that it is his property alone, that it only lives and will live in and by his solace and under his leadership in the expectation of his return."

The unique and gripping note in this is the Evangelical meeting's use of the same biblical passage for the basic concept of the church as Pope Pius XII did in his encyclical: "Christ as the head, the church as the body." However, a careful reading of the explanations of this expression reveals a significant difference. In the Evangelical explanation there is a border which may not be overstepped. The church is the body of Christ. Christ is truly in his church, completely and fully. But there can never be talk of any direct identification of Christ and the church. Christ is the free Lord, who in his unfathomable grace enters into his church and lives there, who in his word and work, as he chastises and resurrects, creates life out of the dead, erects his rule in the midst of a world of sin in spite of death and the devil. All this comes through the Holy Spirit in the word and the sacrament.

The church is not only an invisible "spiritual" fellowship, but a visible entity, as visible as that assembly of men which gathers about the word and the sacraments. "But a building, a preacher, a Bible, and an assemblage still does not create a church and a witness. All this will become a church and a witness only when God in his Spirit enters the scene," says a Reformed theologian.

"Let there be no doubt that where baptism and the gospel are, there are the saints," says Luther. For God's word is never ineffective. Where the gospel is truly heard, there the Spirit is at work, and there is a fellowship created which is the church. The church *is* not Christ, but wherever the living Christ speaks and works, there *is* his church. According to Luther, to believe in the church and the communion of saints means: "I believe that there is upon earth a holy assembly and congregation of pure Saints, under one head, even Christ, called together by the Holy Ghost in one faith, one mind and understanding, with manifold gifts, yet one in love. . . . I also am a part and member of the same, a participant and joint owner of all the good it possesses, brought to it and incorporated into it by the Holy Ghost. . . ." (*The Large Catechism.*)

The church has its signs. It has its voice, and it has its acts: Baptism and Holy Communion. In these signs Christ is real and immanent in his church. "The Church is the congregation of saints in which the Gospel is rightly taught and the Sacraments rightly administered," says the Augsburg Confession. Where this happens, there by God's grace and power is the true church, because there is Christ himself with all his saving and creative power. In one of his writings Luther names as signs of the church the following: the Word of God, Baptism, the Eucharist, the power of the keys, i.e., confession and absolution, the office of preaching, prayer in which we publicly praise and thank God, the cross, and suffering.

The church can never become completely and absolutely static. It is always something that happens. It is that place upon this old world where the new world, the kingdom of God, is constantly breaking through the old world's *sacro egoismo,* where all human pride is broken. But it is also the place where mercy breaks through to the poor, the humble, and the despised and where sins are forgiven. Here true fellowship is created between men no matter how different they are. Here is atonement both between God and man and between men. And also between churches!

The church is the working place of the Holy Spirit on earth. It was born in the miracle of Pentecost and will live until Christ comes again to establish the Kingdom in all its visible glory. It is the "place" and the "organ" of the kingdom of God here on earth. It does not stand as a fellowship of particularly dedicated or particularly religious men but a community of brothers, i.e., of ordinary men of the world who through the atonement and resurrection in Christ have been set free to live together in the genuine fellowship for which God has created man, but which sin has destroyed.

The church is not something separated and unique in this world; rather it is this world, with its created men, with its fields and forests, with its work and strain, with life in family and position, but also this world in its fall and sin—brought back by Christ to God. In the church the beginning of the new world takes place here and now. It is not itself the kingdom of God, but it exists for the sake of that kingdom. It has its constant limits in the kingdom of God but also its content and secret as well.

Through this the church is seen as an eschatological magnitude. It points beyond itself to that kingdom that is yet to come. It appears in this world in hiddenness and ambiguity, always under "the sun of Satan," tempted to apostasy and emancipation and yet under God's mighty promise. God himself will accomplish his kingdom, that kingdom of which the church is the beginning. This is the place of the church in the great drama of the kingdom, as a link in God's plan of salvation. It is a realization of God's plan "according to his purpose which he set forth in Christ as a plan for the fulness of time, to unite all things in him, things in heaven and things on earth" (Eph. 1:9-10).

The crucified and risen Christ, living and immanent through the Holy Spirit in the word and sacrament, freely and mercifully enters into his created and fallen humanity and acts as Lord. In atoning and redeeming and destroying the work of the devil, he creates the new world with that "one new man." He does so even here and now to the glory and praise of his name. So reads the letter to the Ephesians—that one letter of the New Testament which more than any other deals with these things.

In this basic view much of Roman and Evangelical theology can join in a common "yes." But the ways separate the moment there is talk of how this is realized in the church.

Chapter 5

FAITH AND GRACE

Before continuing with the question of the church and its means of grace—the word and the sacraments—we must first concern ourselves with one of the points in the relationship between Romans and Protestants which has perhaps been the source of the widest rift from the very beginning. It has given birth to innumerable polemical writings and controversies as well as to misunderstandings and distortions. Hardly any point has been the occasion for so many slogans which have often threatened to obscure completely what the issue actually was.

How often one has heard that Romans hold that we are saved by "good works" while Protestants rely upon God's grace! The air has swarmed with half-truths or completely undigested fragments of truth: works-righteousness and faith-righteousness, faith and works in opposition to faith alone. Both sides have pictured grim bogeymen against whom it was not too difficult to give stalwart blows.

Consequently there is hardly any place where it is as necessary to clarify the concepts as here. Here where we are concerned with man's relationship to God the old, unyielding, closed, and stagnated formulas will not help us in the slightest to reach any real understanding. Such sketchy abstractions do not really clarify the matter at all, because they simply do not touch the real contradiction between Roman and Evangelical Christians. The following brief explanation of this question cannot claim to unsnarl this tangle of threads. That would require a much longer and deeper investigation. What we shall try to do is briefly sketch the general picture, the two different perspectives, or the two different dimensions, out of which contexts the various words receive their meaning. It's common knowledge that the same word may have completely different meanings depending entirely upon the circumstances in which it is used. In this way words such as faith, grace, sin, revelation, and salvation have a different ring depending upon the general view in which they have their place.

Previous chapters concerned the level or horizontal line so to speak: the tradition down through the ages; the church as the place where God continuously makes real his salvation. But here we are concerned with the perpendicular, the vertical line: the relationship between God and man. What is salvation? What is faith? What is the content of the gospel previously mentioned, that truth which is entrusted to the church and which the church is charged with learning and proclaiming? Could there be a relationship between the contradiction described in the two previous chapters and that which we meet here—and which has a clear influence on what will be discussed in the following chapter about the church's means of grace?

We will describe that view primarily by following one particular theologian—the renowned Thomas Aquinas (d. 1274). We do not arbitrarily choose him from among many Roman theologians. We choose him because he is the church father which the Roman church itself considers as the greatest and the most "authentic" in defining the

Roman position. We will proceed on the basis of Thomas' great dogmatics, *Summa Theologica*. What does it have to say about our subject: Faith and Grace?

Summa Theologica consists of three main parts. The first section concerns God, the beginning and end of all things, the proofs for his existence, his triune nature, his works of creation, and primarily the crown of his creativity: mankind.

The second and by far the largest section deals with humanity, with man's nature, with his intelligence and will, with all his works, primarily those acts that are unique to man in contrast with the rest of the creation. Here man is pictured as the free, personal being who always strives for a goal, and who by God's grace has also been set upon the way toward his eternal goal, the blessed vision of God in eternity. The third part considers Christ and the sacraments as those means whereby man is restored in order to take the road back to God, our final and only goal. In this disposition we are given aid from the very beginning in understanding the Roman Catholic "dimension," and it is this which we will now to try to explore a little more thoroughly.

Thomas poses this question: *What is the final end of man?* Not honor, wealth, or on the whole his desire for anything created, but rather eternal life or to behold the Lord. In this every man's desire is fulfilled. According to Thomas this means that man has a *double* end, in part the natural, which corresponds to his created nature, and in part the supernatural, which God in his love gives to man. Mankind is then first and foremost nature. That is, he was created in a very distinct place in the great order of existence, just on the border between the material and the spiritual world. Man is, it is said, a reasoning being, a body equipped with reason, with freedom, with will, and with an ambition to realize his own nature.

But God was not content only to create man as nature, that is, with all the natural faculties and qualities which peculiarly belong to man and without which he would not be a man but an animal. God gave us from the beginning something infinitely higher, an aim to strive for far beyond the limits and claim of our nature. He gave us a goal which means not only reaching the full potential of natural qualities and faculties but the raising of these same qualities and faculties infinitely beyond themselves. And God not only gave the goal but also the power to reach it. If my natural reason is capable of knowing that God exists and of knowing a little about who he is, then nature is now so elevated as to be able to know God in his own inner supernatural divinity. And if my natural will is capable of striving for a natural good and must necessarily do that, then my will is now so elevated as to be able to strive toward God as my highest end, to love God not only with a natural love but with a supernatural love, even that love with which God loves himself in the inner perfect life of the Holy Trinity. There is no contradiction between the natural end and this supernatural end, because the supernatural life grafts itself upon the natural. Adam was created in this way, not only as a natural man but also a participant in God's own divinity, as a creature who by the goodness of God was exalted to life together with God himself.

This divine power by which nature unceasingly transcends itself and becomes a participant in the divine nature is called grace by Roman Catholicism. Grace is a supernatural, created, divine power through which human nature is fulfilled far beyond its natural capacities and powers. As Thomas himself expresses it, it is the deification of man. This does not mean that the distinctions between God and man are erased, but it does mean that by grace man is made partaker of the divine nature, and man thereby becomes capable of accomplishing supernatural deeds and is led forward toward the supernatural end that God provides.

Adam lived in this spiritual life with God, but the fearful thing happened that, in his freedom, man transgressed God's law for his life and so lost the supernatural grace. This meant a catastrophe for all of humanity. What now remained of humanity? What is the condition of man who by his sin has lost God's grace, whose nature no longer participates in God's nature, whose reason no longer recognizes God, whose will no longer loves God, and who is now inclined toward that which is worldly and sensual? According to the opinion of some Roman theologians, man reverts to his pure human nature. According to others (including Thomas Aquinas) this nature has suffered severe damage by disobedience and the fall through sin. In the consideration of this problem at the Council of Trent it was first proposed to state that no portion of the human soul remained undamaged by sin. This did not happen. Instead the council agreed to use the expression that Adam by sin was "changed for the worse" in respect to both his body and soul. The important council thus took a middle position between Thomas, who regarded the fall of sin as a basic damage also to the natural man, and those theologians who maintained that man's human nature remains undamaged after the fall.

However this is resolved—and the debate in this respect is often very subtle—there is always, according to the

Roman conception, a natural striving upon which grace can build and into which grace may be grafted. Man in his reason and his will is in a "relationship of obedience" to God; that is, man is capable of being raised up to the supernatural life with God. The natural image of God is preserved and is a condition of the work of grace by which the supernatural image of God can again become a reality. Actually this is what salvation consists of, that God in his revelation in Christ and through the means of grace of the church gives man the sanctifying grace by which man becomes able to participate in the spiritual life in faith, hope, and love. In this manner man is able to move forward toward his eternal goal, life in blessedness with God.

Let us try to express this a little differently. According to the Roman conception, man may be comparable to a vessel destined for and also capable of being filled to a constantly higher and higher degree with the divine content—to become holy. Man is—to express it a little more philosophically—a form of being capable of being filled with a higher potentiality, God's own supernatural, holy existence. A stone is so limited by its own closed existence that it cannot become anything more. But a man is not so closed—indeed is just the opposite. By virtue of his own nature—a body determined by and formed by an immaterial soul with its faculties, intellect, and will—he is capable of receiving a high existence, destined more for God's immense spiritual world than material things. Man has the possibility, if God so wills and in his grace so grants, to be filled with God's own nature, that is to say with grace. Roman authors describe this with great exuberance and enthusiastic arguments. God is the infinite fulfilment of

existence; man is the infinite potentiality who may thereby
be filled. Grace is like an infinite stream of love into man,
the new *eros,* the new great strong will, the new fulness of
God (Karl Adam).

By grace the new and true "superman" is created, the
saint who is completely filled with God. Grace, says
Thomas, is a "sort of perfection which elevates the soul
to some supernatural existence." Man is incapable of mov-
ing forward toward his goal without grace. By himself
man is nothing, but by the help of divine grace he earns
not only the constant increase of grace but also—finally—
eternal life. Thomas often speaks of merits—never of man's
own merits—but always as the fruit of the implanting of
divine grace. This last expression is peculiar to the Roman
interpretation. Grace is something divine that flows into
humanity, something which is implanted, which grows,
which departs, is lost and is regained anew. It becomes
very natural to speak of it in the categories of nature,
which must not be misunderstood in such a way that it
becomes a "physical" entity. It is a spiritual reality throughout that belongs to human reason, will, and heart. Nevertheless these pictures of a stream or a grafting serve best
in its description, because grace is really conceived of as a
divine power which is infused in man. In our consideration
of the sacraments we will have opportunity to probe into
this further.

In the meantime this raises a question: Does this then say
that grace as Thomas conceives of it does not mean that
God forgives the sinner? But it does also mean this, and
this naturally plays a very large role. Nevertheless it is
wrong to say that the forgiveness of sin is the essential and
primary work of grace, but is rather a provisional or tem-

porary task. According to Thomas its essential function
is in its work of "elevation," whereby human nature is made
participant in the divine and holy life. Thomas does not
hesitate to call this sanctification a deification. Its task is
to fill the "vessel of nature" with supernatural content, to
help mankind to a spiritual, holy life here on earth, whose
end is eternal life with the blessed vision of God, where
God completely and directly makes his home in man.

This entire view depends upon a very definite concept
of man. Mankind does not confront God first and foremost
as a sinner, so judged by God's living word. Such was the
situation as seen by the Reformers, and to this we shall
shortly return. Man is seen primarily as "nature" which to
be sure—measured by that lost, supernatural, "original justice"—is "changed for the worse," but who has not in himself suffered any damage. Man has lost that sanctifying
grace and has thereby been deprived of supernatural gifts.
Man has also "greed" within himself, by which is understood that constant downward pull of the higher man by
the lower man. But this covetousness is in itself not sin,
although it can become a very dangerous prelude to sin. In
this connection the decisive thing is that man is first and
foremost seen as the "natural" man, strangely "shielded"
from the claims of God's law. It would seem that this concept of man as the "neutral-natural" roots in the Greek,
especially the Aristotelian way of thinking. From this
source it has penetrated the Christian thought world where
it plays a decisive role in the view of man.

On this basis it is also possible to understand what is
meant on Thomistic grounds by the concept of revelation.
This is related to and bears the stamp of the entire philosophy of "potentiality."

God is. God is eternal, exalted over all nature. He is the supernatural triune divinity, perfect, limitless, infinite. Revelation then means that this God unveils the depths of his own nature, his divine nature, for man so that man may again participate therein. At the same time God reveals those means whereby he will lead men back to himself and their supernatural end. However it is not possible for God to reveal himself directly, because no created being is strong enough to behold God, even as the weak eyes of the bat cannot tolerate the direct light of the sun without being completely blinded. The distance is too great. As long as we are here upon this earth, God must reveal his own nature indirectly in concepts and statements that are accessible to human perception, to the human intellect. Those statements, formulated in human language, expressing in part God's inner divinity and in part the means God uses to bring man back to himself, are called dogmas. A dogma is thus a supernatural truth which is revealed by God, and contained in tradition or in scripture taught by the church for faith. These doctrines do not exhaust completely the essential divine reality, but here on earth they are the infallible statements concerning this reality.

Men must accept in faith this revelation which meets them not only in dogma but throughout the entire teaching work of the church. Faith is the human intellect's assent and acceptance of dogma as God's truth, not because it has seen God himself, but because it is convinced that this is the way it is, even though it cannot itself see through the matter. Let us take a very crude example. A good friend comes home from a foreign part of the world and tells of the strange and marvelous but, in and of themselves, unbelievable things there. I have myself neither seen nor experienced these things and my reason can hardly comprehend their truth. What then? My friend, an absolutely trustworthy person, tells this to me. Then my will also goes to work and says to my intellect: "To be sure you cannot understand it, but as he is a trustworthy man and as it is therefore right to accept his words as truth, you must give your consent to this and be certain that it is true."

If this is true in respect to a person, how much more true it must be when it is the almighty God who reveals not merely something incidental but something that is of infinite good for man, something which man in his innermost being longs for most—namely, eternal life. You shall give your consent, says the will which is moved by God's grace to reason, and reason bows itself and gives its unqualified consent. This consent is only possible by virtue of the grace.

The act of believing is therefore an act of the intellect, assenting to divine truth at the command of the will, moved by the grace of God. Its final basis is that it is God himself who speaks. I believe in God's authority. But I do not blindly believe. My reason does have a certain knowledge that these things which are presented for acceptance by faith are trustworthy and not meaningless.

Practically speaking it is on the authority of the church that I believe these things and the church is in itself, in its history, with its saints, in its unity, strength, and beauty an extremely important and trustworthy witness. And as we know that it is charged by Christ himself to protect and guard the truths and that its teachings are therefore infallible, it is natural that the act of faith can very simply be described in this manner: To believe is to accept what the church teaches. Or: I believe it because the church says it. Between this way of expressing it and the way earlier mentioned: I believe, because God says it—there is in reality no difference. Thomas, however, uses the expression: I believe because God has spoken. With him, the church appears more as one who proposes what shall be believed. The developments of more recent times have tended increasingly in the direction of using the authority of the church in the validation of faith without feeling any contradiction in this to God's authority.

Faith meets these different dogmas as they are contained in the teaching of the church both on the solemn high level of the papal definition of dogma and in the church's common "daily" teachings. These are all necessary for salvation. A Roman Catholic cannot permit himself to deny any one of these without thereby being excluded from the church. One may not say: I believe in the atoning death of Christ and in his resurrection, but I do not believe, for example, in the dogmas about Mary. In this way I show that I do not believe in the right manner but wish to select those teachings that I will accept, and this is in itself a witness to the fact that I have deviated. For this very reason the Mary dogmas, to which we will return later, conclude with a sharp warning to those who might be tempted to resist these or to interpret them in any sense other than that in which they were given by the church. He who would do that must know that he thereby draws upon himself the wrath of the Almighty God and of the holy apostles Peter and Paul. As time goes by there naturally will come more and more dogmas as the church is given more and more insight into the revelation. Every new truth of faith shall be believed with the same trust

with which one believes in Jesus Christ, his cross, and
resurrection. (A dogma is a dogma, that is, a divinely revealed truth, whether it concerns the infallibility of the
pope or the crucifixion of Jesus Christ. Even if there is a
significant difference between these two dogmas, they shall
both nevertheless be believed and be accepted as divinely
true. This is also true of any later dogmas which are still
to be defined by the church.)

A new question now arises: Is this faith as described here
sufficient in and of itself for salvation? We may read time
after time in the New Testament, "Your faith has saved
you." And we know the Pauline expression: "Made righteous through faith." According to the Roman Catholic
interpretation this last expression does not mean that faith
itself makes righteous or saves—or that faith in itself is a
means of receiving salvation. "Made righteous by faith"
means that faith as we have described it is the basis for
justification, is the premise of it, as its root and its beginning. It belongs—as far as adults are concerned—to the
preparation, to the entering into justification.

Faith can very well exist before justification; it can also
be found in a man who has lost the grace which makes
righteousness and who finds himself in mortal sin. Justification itself takes place in an area other than faith which
after all in itself is "only" the intellectual acceptance of the
supernatural truths of revelation, even if God's grace has
been active in that acceptance. Justification itself, i.e., that
act in which the sanctifying, elevating grace is implanted
in a man and makes him holy and supernatural, takes place
in the sacrament of baptism, or if grace is lost through a
mortal sin, in the sacrament of penance.

In itself, faith is therefore not sufficient for salvation.

Something more is needed and this more which "forms" the faith and makes it perfect is love. Only when love quickens the act of believing, permeating the will and the whole person, can faith become the saving faith. Essentially it would be more true on Roman Catholic grounds to say justified by love than to say justified by faith. For faith is "only" the "yes" of the intellect to the revelation. It is not yet full life with God.

Faith gives the truth concerning God and those means that God has revealed for the salvation of man, but love alone unites man with God. It is also therefore natural— although we can no more than mention it here—that the spiritual life is completed in mysticism, in the lives of the saints, where the triune God will come to man and make his home in the soul, thus communicating himself in a fulness of life that escapes every attempt at description and can only be experienced. But the mystic experiences are in reality that for which every baptized person is destined.

If we should summarize and try to say what is most characteristic of this interpretation of Christianity, we would have to say that Romanism sees the relationship between God and man in the perspective of the natural and the supernatural—that is, in the plan of elevation, by which man through grace becomes capable of life on the spiritual plane—far beyond any capacity of his own nature. When this whole conception of Christianity is sometimes called "legalistic," we do not mean a Christianity of law in a vulgar sense. Naturally this also does exist, but in any case this is not the concept of Thomas Aquinas. We mean rather a Christianity where the central issue is the holiness of humanity understood as its constant fulfilment, its constant "ascent." The law is not an externally commanded law but

in Christianity is really united with grace itself, which gives
the power to fulfil the law's demand for holiness. Christ
and the law have become one in the new covenant, for
which reason the gospel can also be called the new law.
Everything in Christianity and in the sacramental life of
the church is understood within this general view which
also decides the "use" the Roman Catholic church makes
of all the goods of the church.

In sketching the general view of the Evangelicals regarding faith and grace we will confine our discussion, as
in our presentation of the Roman position, mainly to the
ideas of one particular man—Martin Luther. He has not
presented his view in as systematically clear and complete
a fashion as did Thomas Aquinas, but there does lie a very
definite view of faith and grace behind Luther's enormous
production despite its fragmentary character and multi-
plicity which does not allow itself to be systematically
gathered into a logical whole free from any contradictions.
The matter was very clear and remained constant for Luther
throughout his life.

If anyone were to ask how Luther actually arrived at the
evangelical viewpoint which led him in the opposite direction from the Roman church of his day, I would answer: In
the final analysis that is a secret, God's secret with that
man whom he chose to carry out a work in the church.
But as this is said, we must also add that Luther's view was
naturally prepared for through others and was influenced
by their thoughts about Christianity. And an essential part
of the answer is to be found in his intense preoccupation
with the Bible. Here he found a new light which changed
his view of the relationship between God and man and
thereby also of the "use" of the goods of the church of

which we spoke earlier. The Bible has its own voice, its own unique view. Evangelical Christians can only conclude that Luther—without in any way being infallible—did hear the genuine biblical voice and see the point of view of the Bible and let this voice sound forth to the entire church on earth. He was not the only one, but he was perhaps the one who found the greatest clarity on the decisive points.

We begin with two words—law and gospel—which played so great a role in the time of the Reformation itself and which can yet lead us to a genuine understanding. God meets his created man in the law and in the gospel. This means that God meets us as the one sovereign Lord and Creator, the one who has given and who constantly in every moment gives man life with all its content. Life is not something that man himself forms and shapes according to his own will, but life has a law which places man under a responsibility. God demands the whole man. The great command of the law reads: You shall love the Lord your God with all of your heart, and with all of your soul, and with all of your strength, and with all of your mind, and your neighbor as yourself. This is to be understood in a completely literal way.

To know God does not mean to rise up into the heights and meet God in his heavenly majesty, but to meet God in this human life, as he has created it, with its law which bids us to love him in an absolute way. In this relationship "love" does not have anything to do with romantic feelings but is a matter of the will: obedience. Jesus formulated the command in this manner: Be perfect, even as your heavenly Father is perfect. From this perspective Jesus' Sermon on the Mount is in its entirety a vast intensification of the law, an immense development of what it means to deal with God. The Sermon on the Mount does not merely give evangelical advice to individuals but is rather the proclamation to mankind of the kingdom of God's law over life. The law does not only demand external deeds but demands ourselves—with our bodies and our souls.

Mankind was created to belong wholly to God. He was created for obedience, to be with God the Creator in complete openness and joy. He was created to live in complete openness and fellowship with his neighbor. Man was not intended to keep anything for himself, nor reserve himself, but to give himself to God and to his neighbor in love. For this reason the innermost demand of the law is always love. Love means not to be mired in egoism's avaricious self-centeredness. In short, it means to give. Luther does not accept the separation between the natural and the spiritual. God's purpose for man as a created being—with his reason and his will as a whole person—was to live in love toward God, his Creator and Lord, and toward his fellow man, his brother. There was nothing else to be added. Through freedom he should find his life in community with God and fellow man. A "neutral-natural" man who can only be defined as an "animal rationale" has no real meaning in this connection. God has given man his reason and his will in order that he might therewith serve, know, and obey God and be lord upon the earth together with his fellow creatures, most of all his brothers and sisters. Without reason, man is not man. Reason is God's great gift to man and through his reason man should recognize God in his works toward him and thereby grow in obedience toward him. Reason has received all its light from God in order to know and to understand.

For Luther, the fall means that this original, natural relationship with God has completely fallen to pieces. According to the Evangelical conception, it is incorrect to say that man has kept his nature intact after the fall, as some Roman theologians express it. But it is no more correct to speak of an impaired nature. Neither of these answers penetrate to the core of the matter. Luther would surely say that man has retained both his reason and his will, considered as neutral and "ontological" entities. But of what benefit are these gifts when the person who is to use them does not remain as he was before, but has completely changed? This is not the place to enter a discussion of how, much less when, this happened. We know nothing about that. The significant thing is that we find here another concept of the relationship between man and God than in our sketch of the Roman Catholic view. What has happened, or, more correctly, what is it that constantly happens in our persons, that is to say, in that "I" which lies behind our entire lives as men, that has made us what we are? This is where Luther begins. And here he probes deeper than most.

Luther does not say that man is no longer man as some have accused him of saying. He does say that the human person no longer lives in obedience, openness, and joy under and together with God, its creator, and he no longer loves his fellowman as himself. To say it another way: man was destined to live in faith, that is, to receive everything from God, to live with God in trust, and thankful openness. This is no longer true. Instead, in a strangely distorted manner, man lives in unbelief. Man is turned toward himself and no longer toward God or toward his fellow man. He has the iron band of isolationism around his heart. His will is no longer open and willing to serve others and his reason is no longer turned toward God. Rather he uses his reason not only to perceive the outer world but also to serve the "I," to secure and entrench the "I," to build great systems through which he can make himself the lord of all existence and "capture" the living God in his own net. He even—and Luther considers this the most serious—seeks to use reason to justify himself both before God and his fellow man and also before himself. The person of man becomes a jack-of-all-trades in order to find excuses and in order to "clear himself," and for this purpose he uses his reason.

This is why Luther denounced reason in many places—not because he hated reason. He acknowledges it highly as God's good gift to man without which man would not be capable of understanding anything, least of all God's own words to us. But his strong words apply to reason used as a servant of the "I." Through the strength of his reason, man's mightiest weapon in his battle for himself, he often builds a fortress against God. Luther saw in reason a servant who could fulfil the command to make the whole world subservient to man. This was only good. But he also saw how man by virtue of his reason isolated himself from the living God and built up his own life with the "I" at the center.

This is moreover one of the reasons that Luther turns in wrath against the Aristotelian philosophy. It is not that he has anything against Aristotle as a philosopher—philosophically speaking, he may very well have been Aristotelian in his own thinking. It was rather Aristotle's influence in theology, in Christian thinking, that aroused him, because man could make himself secure in this world by the strength of Aristotle's immense thought system. Everything was put in its place and a balance established between man and God which simply did not exist. God was naturally part of the system but only in his specific place therein. Then God was really no longer God but only an idol who was created in the image of man. Aristotelian philosophy prevented man from acknowledging God as the true Lord of life with his inexorable demands upon his creation, because it knocked the corners off and gave to man a kind of a natural God who was, in the final analysis, in man's own pocket.

We find something here which it is necessary to try to understand if we are concerned with how Luther regards man and his relation to God. It is not only important for the Catholic who seeks to understand Luther but it is also necessary for the Evangelical Christian who, time and again, is tempted to forsake this view because it is too harsh and has so strong a head wind that he longs for more comfortable and milder breezes.

Man is never outside the law of God. Where the law meets a man in all seriousness, there he recognizes God's inescapable majesty, what sin is, and what he is himself. Then man may be tempted to revolt against God. Or something else can happen: man acknowledges that God is right. Then man learns something about who God is. He does not learn by climbing up some steep, metaphysical ladder or by some mystical experiences. But he learns through the seriousness of his own life here on earth out of which situation it is absolutely impossible to lift himself a fraction of an inch.

The recognition of the God of law is at the same time the recognition of sin. In these circumstances, the acknowledg-

ment of sin is not the same as the moral consciousness of
guilt which man feels when he sees the distance between
himself and the goal or ideal at which he aimed. The
recognition of sin comes when man sees himself in the light
of the law's absolute claim concerning love of the *entire*
heart for God and his fellow man. This has nothing to do
with either hysteria or pessimism, nor with a moral, matter-
of-fact argumentation. Man becomes able to "see" himself
in a new manner. The law is no more a moral lever which
is a beginning for that trek toward the heights. The law
has become a killing power in the life of created man.

Great men in the history of the church have all been
aware of this. Here man is out in the depths, far beyond
those little water puddles of moralism where it is still possible to paddle. Sin is not only single sinful actions. These
are only symptoms of something that goes deeper, of something that is within the "person," within the "I" itself. For
this reason Luther also calls sin in its very essence the sin
of the person. Sin is to will oneself in opposition to God
and to one's fellow man. Man is no longer open but
strangely perverted into himself. That is not only true in
coarse and obvious matters but also in the finer and more
spiritual areas, even where a man is most "religious." The
more invisible the poison gas is, the more dangerous it is.
And it is most dangerous when man uses God as a tool of
his own will to seek his own fortune by means of his religion, and thus even more fearfully to cut himself off from
community with his fellow man. Religion is not a sanctuary
where sin does not have access. Just the opposite. Men
have become idolaters even in the relationship to God
which is seemingly deepest.

When a man knows what this means, or begins to sense

it, he also knows something about judgment. In the explanation to the second article of faith in the small catechism, Luther uses the phrase, "Me, a lost and condemned creature." This is not an expression of a hysterical and pessimistic conception of man. Luther knew very well that man has the capability and responsibility of doing something good in his worldly relationships. For that purpose, man also has a measure of free will. What Luther does say is that when a man confronts God's unqualified demand that he be good to the roots of his being, that he love God and his neighbor with all of his heart and so give himself, then he stands as one condemned. Then he is done for as a man. We repeat: It could not occur to Luther for one moment that man should not have all his natural endowments intact. Man has not degenerated to something "sub-human," still less to an animal state. But of what benefit to man are all these endowments of reason and will when the person who is to use these higher things is as he is? According to this view reason and will are not positive points of contact with something higher, much less with something supernatural. It is doubtful then if there is any meaning in speaking of man in even a completely passive "potential of obedience" toward God in such a way that reason and will in their natural "neutral" condition can be considered the natural soil of the spiritual life. It is as if the words in this perspective receive another meaning.

To confront the God of the law is not to face a list of legal paragraphs which we eventually all transgress, but to meet a living reality, a holiness, before which man stands guilty and condemned. Man does not appear here as one who is striving upward, who is helped onward by the law, but here man appears as that creature whose very existence is threatened. Here he is not the natural man who in his nature is a fertile soil for supernatural growth. Here is a creature who has not fulfilled the Creator's intent with his life and is therefore at odds with his own destiny.

Nevertheless, this man is the man that God created in his own image for fellowship with him and his neighbor, created to live in the kingdom of God. The fact that man cannot live without God shows itself in many ways: in the abundance of religions, man's longings and aspirations; in the absence of peace, his anxiety. At one and the same time man is God's own creation and is in flight from God—destined to be a child of God and yet a rebel—provided with gifts no other creature on the face of the earth has received, and yet one who misuses and perverts the high gifts he possesses. Man is thus under the judgment of God. This is the word of the law to man. A person can neglect God's law in rebellion and defiance. He can "abolish" God. In our time, few have predicted this possibility as well as Nietzche and Dostoevsky who thereby touched upon the deepest level of man's "potentiality." Or man can whittle down the law, make it into civil law so that it becomes practicable and manageable. But he is thereby making himself immune to God, for the law of God is in this way neither practicable nor manageable. Or a man can take the law into his own hands and with its help try to justify himself before God as a pious man who thinks that he has something to offer God! The religious man nevertheless often thinks in terms of merits, even if it would never occur to him to use that word. Luther often used the word *justitiarius*, meaning the religious man who tries to reach the living God by the means and the way of the law.

Or a man may be destroyed by despair, defiance, and rebellion against a God who has arranged life in such a way. In one way this man does admit the law to be right, but it is an admission of despair and hatred of a law that does not save but throws a man into misery.

In this way we have reached the point where we can understand what the word "grace" means for Evangelicals. God's judgment is not God's proper action toward man. It is—to use Luther's own words—God's "alien work." It is not God's nature to judge but to love. It was in his love that the world was created and the will of love is to lead his fallen creation back to him, even to redeem the entire world whose purpose it was to be an expression of God's sovereign kingdom. God's grace is in one single word— Christ. According to the Evangelical view grace is not a divine power, a supernatural form of being, that grafts itself into the nature of man and elevates it into a spiritual form of existence. It is rather God's personal, gracious, merciful love to his fallen creation, made alive and revealed in Christ. Everything is given in him. He is the word of God; that is, the fullest expression of who God is and what God wills.

Christ is the miracle of God, not only in the sense that his person and his life are miraculous, but in a far deeper sense; because a word is heard in Christ that breaks through and overcomes the voice of the law and judgment. In the monastery at Erfurt, Luther was plagued by the question: How shall I find a gracious God? The basic question of man is not only, *is* there a God, but is there a *gracious* God? As long as man remains on the legal basis, the answer remains: Fulfil the demands of the law and you will be righteous before God. But in the gospel—and this word is only another expression for grace and for Christ—the legal basis is penetrated and man confronts that God who freely gives life to man who formerly was judged and under other powers. Grace thus means something absolutely personal, that Christ enters into the broken existence of man and says to God's fallen creation: You are a child of God. You belong to God. In the word grace lies the mighty ring of free pardon, of that miracle that takes place in the fact that the judge himself steps over to the side of the accused and takes up his cause. The strange thing even happens that the judge himself becomes the defender, while the accused becomes the accuser. For the accused must admit the justice of the accusation. Justification—to use the classical expression—is that act, the miracle, that takes place when God in his grace, incarnate in Jesus Christ, completely and fully takes the place of the one who is under judgment and grants him life again by forgiveness.

There is one point that has often been obscured by later Lutheran thinking. It is extremely important to underline the fact that justification, grace, and the gospel, or whatever word one chooses to use, is not something that awaits man at the end of the road when he has worked his way up the ladder of the law. Rather, it is given in personal communion with Christ, who enters personally into the life of sinful man as his Lord and Savior. In communion with him, *everything* is given. "Where there is forgiveness of sins, there is also life and salvation." Or as Luther very clearly expresses it in the explanation to the second article of faith: Everything that Christ has done is done "in order that I may be his."

The miracle of justification lies in man, as a forgiven sinner, becoming God's true and righteous creation, re-

leased to serve and love God and his neighbor in obedience
and faith. Salvation means the redemption and restoration
of the created being, not into some spiritual form of
existence but into the human life which is released from
the stunted and perverted character of sin—to live in fellowship with Christ and his neighbor here on earth as the
true, natural man. And all this is in the hope of the final
victory of the kingdom of God, the hope which the creed
expresses in the words: "the resurrection of the body and
the life everlasting." The design for man's existence is
totally changed—solely by God's gracious intervention.

Throughout this entire view we meet the word "faith."
Faith, according to the Evangelical conception, is that
relationship to God through which alone man receives
salvation. Faith is not just the premise of that reality which
is to follow, but faith contains in itself that new relationship
to God.

In his great commentary on the letter to the Galatians,
Luther says that faith is not a dead thing in man, an empty
shell which can very well exist together with a mortal sin,
and which first receives its meaning when love comes and
gives it warmth. Rather, where there is true faith, there
is a certain trust and secure consent in which Christ is
comprehended and becomes the only object of faith for
"in faith itself, Christ is present."

In this definition there are several things to note. In
the first place, faith does not need to be complemented by
anything else in order to describe the true relationship with
God. In it man meets God himself. This was also the use
of the word in the New Testament both when Jesus said:
"Your faith has saved you," and when Paul uses the word.
Faith is always a personal-existential relationship between

an "I" and a "thou," not only an intellectual assent which can in and of itself exist without the relationship to God himself. A pure and simple intellectual relationship with God could never be called faith by Luther.

This comes forth even more clearly—and this is the second thing that we will note—when Luther says that it is Christ himself who is the object of faith. Christ is a living person, Lord and Savior himself. This is significant for the nature of faith, for then faith cannot be adequately described in terms of an intellectual assent to a series of doctrines that have been revealed by God and defined by the church. In this context the personal relationship to Christ never does appear. There is a great difference between giving assent to a list of truths of revelation and committing one's entire person to Christ. Where the Roman Catholic conception of faith is expressed in phrases having their source in the area of man's intellect, the Evangelicals must state their faith in personal expressions.

Faith does not respond to a list of revealed truths presented by the church but to the gospel of faith that is proclaimed by the church. In the church, a very distinct proclamation is heard, whose content is Christ himself. This message is distinguished from all other messages in that it concerns the entire existence of man as we have just described it. When man hears this message, he grasps it with his entire heart, with his mind, and with his will or, to mention another insight which Luther greatly emphasized, the message itself grasps man and holds him securely. What takes place here? Here man acknowledges the justice of God's judgment upon him. It is not we who adapt the word to us, but it is the word which adapts us to it, says Luther. For this reason there is always some-

thing in man that is resentful in the encounter with God,
for he does not like to admit the justice of God, but only
his own justice.

Man's sinful will consists of just this, that above all he
wishes to guard himself against God. Man finds it very
difficult by nature to accept that the only possibility for life
is in the fact that God forgives completely. But thereafter
a miracle—and that is what faith essentially is—takes place.
Man simply receives that word or message which alone
resurrects the existence of man from despair. Viewed from
this side, faith is only to receive that pardon in thankfulness, in the same way that the doomed man who is pardoned can only receive his acquittal.

Faith appears in complete contradiction to every idea of
human performance or work. Faith directs itself toward
God's work alone. That is, its only content is Christ. And
let us repeat this one more time: the content of faith is not
first and foremost a teaching about Christ, not the preaching of Christ alone, not his moral example, but very simply
Christ himself. This is the mystery of faith which we cannot logically explain, because it belongs together with the
faith of the church that Jesus Christ truly is, and lives as an
immanent Lord and Savior in our midst. But we know this
Lord through the confession of his apostles, through the
Gospels, and through the apostolic letters. Faith is directed
toward this biblical, present, and living Christ. In fact, in
faith we are united with him and receive therein everything
that is necessary for life and blessedness.

How does Luther describe the act of faith? It is clear
that it is always the object which determines the act. If the
object is the doctrines of the church, then faith must
essentially be an intellectual act, even if this may be dif-

ferent from the natural intellectual acts of man. But if the
object of faith is the living Christ, then we will have to
explain it in another manner. In the above-mentioned
quotation from Luther's commentary on the letter to the
Galatians, Luther uses two expressions. Faith is a "secure
trust" and a "firm consent." When the act of faith is to be
defined on Evangelical terms, the word "trust" is the most
often used. "I dare to place my trust in the only, invisible,
almighty God," says Luther.

Trust is candid and unreserved reliance upon God's
righteousness and the relevance of his word to every man.
It is a completely personal concept expressing the fact
that man dares to renounce himself and his own security,
such as it is, and dares to receive life from the hand of
God. Through trust, man receives something which he
does not have, something that lies beyond what can be
rationally or empirically proven. Trust is a relationship
between persons, and does not belong in an abstract and
intellectual sphere.

But it would nevertheless be a grave misunderstanding
of the Evangelical concept of faith if we were to conclude
that faith has no intellectual aspect. Faith is also assent.
The trust of faith does not vaguely direct itself out into the
blue, is not a blind prayer of the heart or an emotionally-
defined experience. It addresses itself toward a distinct
person, toward Christ, even as the apostolic message proclaimed him in the primitive church. Faith in the evangelical sense is always faith in this Christ. Consequently,
faith is also an enlightenment of man's reason through the
Holy Spirit that he might acknowledge who Christ is. Faith
is never without doctrine about Christ. Evangelical Christianity is not a sort of anti-intellectualism in the sense that

man's comprehension should be minimized. Luther never spoke in this manner. On the contrary: through faith a broadening of man's comprehension takes place which surely cannot be without influence in his relationship to that world in which he must live.

Is man passive in this faith? If the question concerns how far man cooperates in his own salvation, the answer must be yes. That is God's work alone. If the question is rather to what extent faith is a passive and dead acceptance then the question is completely without meaning. God will see to it that it does not become something passive. Faith is not an act in which man is some kind of a wooden block which is not even aware when the axe strikes it. I am afraid that on this point Lutheran theology has often expressed itself in a way that has caused a great degree of misunderstanding, but, as far as I can see, Luther himself never did this. Man is active in faith to a high degree. It could not be otherwise, for nothing less takes place here than that Christ, through faith, gives himself to man. There arises a new fellowship between Christ and man. But fellowship is only possible where both persons participate. In that moment when a man's existence is completely changed through faith, something *happens* in and for him.

Here Roman theology has often misunderstood the Evangelical point of view. The accusation has been made that, according to the Evangelicals, righteousness is nothing more than an "imputed" righteousness, which does not penetrate into the person but only clothes the man as a coat. It is laid upon him without having the slightest consequence in him. God's justification of man thereby becomes something "immoral" and "dishonest." "The divine life does not become a living reality within the soul but can pictorially be compared with that fine glare of light in the polar regions which lies as a veil over the rocks without penetrating them, without allowing itself to be absorbed. The rock is ever cold, hard, dark, and barren as a soul in the grip of sin. Proudly it raises itself out of the ocean but it is unresponsive to the heavenly caress."

This cannot possibly be accepted as a correct description of the Evangelical position. God forgives sinners. This must be understood absolutely literally, and if this were not true, then everything else would be vain. This forgiveness has its root and its power in God's mercy alone, in his grace. That man whose sins are forgiven by God remains a sinner as long as he is on this earth. But he is not an unconcerned sinner for whom everything remains as it was. No, there are truly new things that take place. Luther used the beautiful picture of the twilight, where light and darkness battle. It can be the twilight of the dying day where the darkness is victorious over the light and the night descends. But it can also be the twilight of the dawn where light has its victory over darkness, and the blessed day breaks forth.

This latter is the case. Sin and all the old nature of this old world are defeated, and even though the darkness is still in evidence and constantly threatens and affects man, the new world in which the pardoned sinner has his home has broken through. This is the truth of the Lutheran expression to which Roman Christians react so strongly and so often dispute, that the Christian man is at the same time righteous and sinner.

God's forgiveness in Christ constantly breaks through anew in human existence. This leads us to the final insight into faith—its orientation to the future. The Christian

knows that written across the entire Christian life as well
as over the life of the church is the inscription "not yet."
Therefore, faith lives in the hope that God will fulfil his
redemptive work throughout his entire creation. When a
man looks at himself and thinks of his own salvation, he
has an uncertain and flickering view, but in faith God gives
to man the certainty that what the Almighty has begun he
is also capable of fulfilling. This is the real content of the
certainty of faith. Luther distinguishes clearly between
securitas which means confidence and infers the idea of
self-assurance which is absolutely contrary to the nature
of faith, and *certitudo*—certainty which directs the view
toward God alone, his power and will, which will fulfil his
work.

But what then about all those so-called good works?
We will try to summarize the Evangelical view as briefly
as possible. That faith which we have talked about above
does not live by love's good works, but it lives in them.
Faith lives exclusively by that which God has done and
does in Christ. It is ever receiving. But this faith is not a
static or a lazy thing. It must always go out of its way in
love's service toward its neighbor. Luther expressed this
very paradoxically in this manner: "If faith is not without
even the smallest work, it does not justify, it is on the whole
no faith." But he immediately added, "Faith cannot exist
at all without ever greater and living works. As Christ
descended down from his heaven to become our neighbor,
so are we to live our life with our neighbor." Luther also
wrote, "We shall be a Christ to our neighbor." If it is true,
as we have tried to describe it above, that it is Christ himself who is present in faith, then this must mean that Christ
has become the Lord of life.

Justification also means renewal in the fact that the Christ who is our only righteousness is also the one who becomes the Lord of all life. This received a valid and strong expression at the Lutheran-Reformed Synod of Barmen in 1934. The second thesis of this conference reads: "As Christ is God's promise of the forgiveness of all our sins, He is also, and with the same seriousness, God's vigorous demand upon our entire life. Through Him we are released from all false enchainment to this world to free and thankful service to His creation." "Faith is a living, persevering, working, and mighty thing, so that it is impossible that it is not incessant in its good works. It does not ask if there are good works to do, but before one can ask, it has done them and it is always active" (Luther).

With this we bring this section to a close. It is without doubt one of the most difficult, because here we have been concerned with that which is the most personal of all, the relationship to God. It is also difficult because the boundary between the two conceptions is not established in final and absolute formulas but is in constant flux. And it often cuts across all confessional dividing lines. The goal has been to sketch the two general views and to give an impression of how the words faith and grace have different contents in these two perspectives.

Chapter 6

MEANS OF GRACE AND
THE WORSHIP OF THE CHURCH

What is the essential task of the church? Roman Catholicism answers: to sanctify men. Naturally the church shall also rule, lead, and communicate the complete truth, but these functions are only means for the most important task: sanctification. In this manner the judicial offices, the ministry, and the multifarious external functions may be seen in a new light. In the final analysis they have no goal in themselves but are tools of the church in its most important responsibility, to dispense sanctifying grace to mankind. This was also the central work of Christ.

What is holiness? One of Germany's great Roman Catholic theologians of recent times says that we call the good holy, but the good in an absolutely unique firmness, purity, and sublimity. God is the highest good as is therefore holiness itself. As God's express image, Christ is the God-man permeated by holiness, first and last by love which is the deepest reality of holiness. That holiness is transmitted from Christ to men and gives them a share in God's own life. From his life and from his perfect sacrifice upon the cross, sanctifying grace streams down to the church, sufficient to sanctify all of humanity. In Christ that holiness is unlimited. The church is thus that priestly-sacramental, supernatural organism in which Christ is constantly at work and through which he constantly allows holiness, the divine powers of grace, to flow into men. This union with Christ takes place through the sacraments.

A sacrament is a visible, physical sign of which completely natural things such as water, bread, wine, the laying on of hands, oil, and many others form a part. By the power of priestly consecration and execution these are lifted up into a higher plane, are taken out of the profane sphere and become instruments of divine, spiritual power. There are seven sacraments in number: Baptism, Confirmation, the Eucharist, Penance, Ordination, Marriage, and Extreme Unction. These actions are not merely symbolic pictures of something divine, nor are they actions that "accompany" the divine infusion of grace. According to current Roman Catholic conception the sacraments *accomplish* grace. Baptism releases men from the filth and guilt of inherited sin and implants a new divine nature into the soul of man whereby he with all his natural faculties is elevated, "transfigured," to become a real participant in the life of God. Confirmation strengthens the youth with the power of the Holy Spirit so that he becomes a true soldier of Christ. The sacrament of penance confers forgiveness on man and restores him to the state of grace. Those who are called to the work of the priesthood receive through the sacrament of ordination a unique and indelible grace with the power to administer the sacraments in a valid manner. Those who enter into marriage also receive a unique grace with reference to the particular difficulties and blessings of the marriage state. And extreme unction gives strength in the final hours of this earthly life as it prepares men for the last journey.

Who distributes or administers the sacraments? This is done by the legally-ordained priest. Only baptism can be performed by one who is not ordained, although in marriage the "yes" of the parties involved is the essential part of the sacrament. Baptism and marriage are the only sacraments of the seven that, according to the Roman point of view, are valid in the various Protestant churches. In principle, baptism cannot be repeated, therefore those who enter the Roman church from the Evangelical church are not rebaptized. Nevertheless, rebaptism often does take place on the grounds that the person in question may not have been baptized with a rightly-administered baptism. This possibility is circumvented by the so-called conditional-baptism which uses the following words: "If you are baptized, I do not baptize you. But if you are not baptized, I baptize you in the name of the Father, and of the Son, and of the Holy Ghost."

Even if Protestant baptism is valid and through it a man does in principle belong to the Roman Catholic church, nevertheless the gift of baptism can to a limited extent be of value to such a baptized person. Only if such a person changes over to the Roman Catholic church, will he receive this gift in fullest measure.

The five remaining sacraments have no validity outside the Roman church. The Roman priest is a priest not by virtue of his baptism or his faith, his call, or the congregation that has sought him to be its pastor, but exclusively by virtue of his ordination. As in the final analysis it is Christ himself who offers the sacraments and speaks the consecrating words, who makes the sacraments valid and efficacious, there is necessarily a close relationship between the priest and Christ. It is a relationship that no other

Christian can have. Just as baptism gives the human soul an indelible quality, so those who are consecrated to the priesthood by the sacrament of ordination are placed in a class of their own, in a unique state, equipped with a spiritual power to be instruments of the heavenly and spiritual life of the mystical body of Christ.

Their hands alone are consecrated, as the ritual of ordination says, "so that what they bless shall be blessed, and what they sanctify shall be sanctified in the name of Jesus Christ." Therefore those who would live their lives in Christ must go to the priest, as he is the instrument of Christ. Or as Thomas Aquinas elaborates upon this: Just as Christ worked out our salvation as man and as God, so the priest must in a certain way be a man who participates in the divinity of Christ by virtue of a unique power. In brief: in the administration of the holy functions, the priest does not act as the representative of the congregation but in the place of Christ. He represents in his own person Christ himself; he is "a second Christ." He is mediator between Christ and man. There is no way to the divine life in Christ except through the ordained priest. For this reason the Roman priesthood plays a role that can hardly be exaggerated. At almost every significant point of his spiritual development a Christian will find a priest at his side who has received a special power to communicate or increase that grace which is the spiritual life of his soul. The priest attends the believer throughout the entire pilgrimage of his life; he even follows him behind the great curtain.

What qualifications are demanded of a priest? The Roman and the Lutheran church are agreed that the validity of the sacraments does not depend upon the purely personal qualifications of the priest. The Roman church teaches that the sacrament is valid when the priest has the right intention, that is, when he administers the sacrament with the desire to do so as the church would have it done and in accordance with the teaching of the church. Even if he personally is not convinced that the view of the church is correct, if he has the will to administer the sacrament as the church understands it, the sacrament is valid. If, however, he administers the sacrament in deliberate opposition to the intention of the church, then in spite of correct external execution, it is not valid.

The personal unworthiness of a priest does not affect the validity of those acts which he performs because the holiness of the sacraments is not dependent upon the holiness of the person who administers them. Naturally, this does not in any way mean that the Roman church does not lay the greatest weight upon a well-educated, informed, and holy priesthood. Thomas Aquinas wrote that those who were to be mediators between God and His people "must have a good conscience before God and a good reputation among men." A priest according to Pope Pius XI shall have a sublimity of spirit, a purity of heart, and a holiness of life.

What qualifications are demanded of those who receive the sacraments? This particular question became a burning one at the time of the Reformation since the reformers emphasized so strongly the importance of faith. One only needs to recall Luther's explanation of Holy Communion in his small catechism: "Question: Who receives this sacrament worthily? Answer: Fasting and bodily preparation are indeed a good external discipline; but he is truly worthy and well prepared who believes these words, 'given and shed for you, for the remission of sins.' But he who does not believe these words or who doubts, is unworthy and unfit; for the words 'for you,' require truly believing hearts."

To the question of what is demanded from those who are to receive the sacrament, the Roman church answers: No disposition is required from those who are to receive in order for the sacraments to be valid. The sacrament is valid *ex opere operato*, (by virtue of an executed act) that is, by the strength of the correct execution of the ritual of the sacrament. The Roman church says that the sacrament is secured in this way against all subjective conditions which would render its function relative and uncertain. This does not mean, however, that the sacrament is merely a mechanical act which functions magically. Naturally, there is a constant danger in this direction in the Roman conception of the sacrament, but this is not implied in the official Roman teachings. If the person who comes to the sacrament has no desire to open himself to the spiritual gift of the sacrament or is in a state of mortal sin, then he will not receive the blessings of the sacrament—its grace will not penetrate into his soul. If for example a person goes to confession and consciously hides a serious sin, then he does not receive the forgiveness of sins through the absolution of the priest. The more predisposed a person is to receive the sacrament, the more he receives. This corresponds to the theological premise that grace requires the willingness and cooperation of the receiver before it can flow into his soul and there do its sanctifying work. The demand for such a predisposition is needless only at the baptism of children.

In addition to the sacraments instituted by Christ himself, which are necessary for salvation, the Roman church has a long list of acts and things which are similar to sacraments. These so-called sacramentals are things or acts, somewhat modeled upon the sacraments, which the church uses to accomplish, by the strength of its own intercession, sanctifying works, especially of a spiritual nature. These sacramentals need not have been instituted by Christ, but must always be instituted by the church. It may be various consecrations, e.g., of rosaries, crucifixes, pictures, particularly of the Madonna or of the saints, medals, or holy water, through which these things receive a particular power and value. Or it may be acts that are performed or received with a pious mind; either something that is done to the person such as a consecration, or something that the person does, such as making the sign of the cross. The sacramentals take objects or persons out of the profane or out of that curse which rests upon the creation because of the fall of man. For this reason the priests bless the cornerstone of new houses, the bedroom of the new home, farm and barns, automobiles and domestic animals, wells and springs, and today also railroads and telegraphs.

The ordained priest is also regarded as someone unique, aside from the evaluation of his person. An old, probably Bavarian, saying reads: "Our priest is an ass, in spite of holy consecration!" Through the sacraments and the sacramentals, the church sanctifies the entire creation and human life in all its various forms and various periods. The difference between them consists of the sacraments having active power in themselves when they are correctly executed, while the sacramentals are based upon the intercession of the church and the piety with which the individual executes or uses these.

Throughout all this one gets a strong impression of the

high degree to which so many forms of piety are harmonized in this view of Christianity and human life, from the most sublime to the strangely vulgar. A more thorough examination of Roman Catholic piety in the various areas of the Roman world will strengthen this impression. As seen from the outside, the Roman Catholic structure resembles a tremendous complexity that contains the most paradoxical traits—a *complexio oppositorum,* a unity of contradictions. To a certain degree this is the very pride of Catholicism. This indicates, says the Roman Catholic, the degree to which Catholicism is the religion of all humanity. Historians of religion will find in it many strata, all the way from the most primitive religion with its teachings about "mana," the supernatural mystical power that resides in certain things so that they become "taboo" or untouchable, through the Jewish religion of law, to the Hellenistic mystery religions, from a hierarchical religion of authority to the highest summit of mysticism. Roman Catholicism is a religion where there is room for all, from the most naive, even superstitious, to the most highly educated. And it all finds its place within the totality of Catholicism in which Christianity is the ever continuous sanctifying of the natural, the drawing of the natural from the profane, and the elevation of human nature to a new supernatural form of existence.

One thing more must be considered because it has played such a large role in the relationship between Roman Catholicism and Protestantism and historically was the spark that ignited the Lutheran Reformation: the so-called indulgences. The word has its roots in the Latin *indulgentia* which means "remission." This has often been misinterpreted to mean the forgiveness of sins, which is wrong.

Indulgence is not forgiveness of sins but the remission of the temporal punishment which always follows after sin, even after eternal punishment is remitted either in the sacrament of baptism or of penance. These temporal punishments must be endured by man, either here on earth or in purgatory after death.

For example, if we devoutly pray certain designated prayers, perhaps several times or at designated places, the church can grant remission to a person of temporal punishments which would otherwise have to be expiated in purgatory. In Catholic churches one can find small pictures of saints with a note that one who prays the prayer printed with the picture will receive 300 days' indulgence. What does this mean? It means that the church will grant a remission of temporal punishment that it would, by the decision of the church regarding penance, otherwise take 300 days to expiate. This is the partial indulgence.

Complete indulgence means the absolute remission of all temporal punishment. In the so-called Portiuncula Indulgence a person may pray certain designated prayers in Assisi's Portiuncula Chapel on August 2 in the intention of the Holy Father after confession and Holy Communion, and thereby receive complete absolution. This is also the case during a jubilee year.

It is the teaching of the church that the living can accomplish a reduction of the time of expiation for the dead in purgatory. The church has been no more specific than that it is accomplished by intercession. But in this manner there is a constant fellowship between the living and the dead.

It is a dogma that Christ has himself given the church full authority to distribute indulgences and that these are

highly salutary (*salutaris*). Therefore, says the Council of
Trent, indulgences ought to be retained in the church—
sanctioned by the holy councils' authority. The claim that
indulgences can be traced to Christ himself is supported by
reference to the absolute authority which Christ gave to
his apostles (Matt. 16:18). The premise of all this is the
thesaurus eccelesiae, the "treasury of the church," containing surplus good works which Christ and the saints have
wrought. These surplus good works make up a sort of
"family fortune" which belongs to the entire church with
all its members. In a profound sense the doctrine of indulgences does give an expression of the fellowship between the saints and the believing, of the communion of
saints. By virtue of that absolute power given to it by Christ,
the church can now draw from this common treasury and
distribute to all its believers, enabling those who have much
to help those who have but little.

At the time of the Reformation, indulgences were evilly
and grossly misused, because they had become related to
money. This misuse was later abolished by the Council of
Trent. Although money is not absolutely done away with
in relation to indulgences, care must be taken "that the
alms and the love-gifts that are given in this connection are
never considered as payments or that any credit is gained
in this manner. One must ultimately understand that this
heavenly treasury of the Church does not exist for the sake
of income but shall exclusively serve the cause of piety."
Indulgences do not belong to the sacramental life of the
church but are rather a function of the church as the
spiritual judge over all men. It is the pope and the bishops
who, as the sovereigns of the church, are possessors of the
full power to distribute indulgences. The extent to which

the bishops can distribute these is carefully determined by canon law. The unavoidable central principle is that this distribution must serve a religious purpose. Otherwise, it is not valid.

In the discussion of the Roman mass we will return to the question of the church's priestly-sacramental function. But what is the Evangelical Lutheran view of those things which we have been discussing? It will already be understood that there is an essential contrast in these matters between the Roman Catholic and the Evangelical views. This does not exclude the fact, however, that there is also, in spite of all, a common ground which it is significant to underscore.

When the Roman Catholic church says that God's salvation comes to us through external things, through words and acts, when it says that God does not give of himself directly to the individual apart from the church which Christ instituted, then there is no disagreement between Romans and Evangelicals. If we go back to Luther, we will discover that he earnestly combats those who speak of the Spirit as something which is, so to speak, floating free in the air, which comes unconditionally to all men. No, God's work and the immanence of Christ in our midst are knit to definite external things, to things corporate and tangible.

Just as God comes to us in Jesus as a man of flesh and blood, he also comes to us now in physical things, in a word that can be heard or an act that can be seen. For this reason Luther battled the fanatics and those whom he called the enthusiasts, who denied the visible signs and who said that one needed only to believe. On the contrary, faith does have something to stand securely upon, the

word which is proclaimed and heard, the external signs of
Baptism, Holy Communion, Confession and Absolution.
One may never separate faith from the external, nor belittle those outward things to which faith clings and without which it cannot rise and cannot live. Christianity is
something that comes to me, not something that arises
within me. For this reason, when the church was defined
for us as a community of brothers in which Christ himself
acts in the present as Lord, through the Holy Spirit, in
word and sacrament, this was an authentic Evangelical
explanation. Evangelical Christianity is not to be found
on a plane where everything is spiritualized, where externals
play no role but are set aside as things that belong to a
lower type of religion which has no meaning for man
today.

It is against this common background that the differences
show up so clearly. In contrast with the Roman Catholic,
the concept of the Evangelical church appears first of all
as a great simplification. The apparatus of the church has
become much smaller. Some Protestants would maintain
that the church has been greatly impoverished, others will
argue that the Evangelical Lutheran church is still far
too complex! For the Reformers the question was not a
quantitative one, of more or less. They were concerned
with something much more essential—the problem of restoring original Christianity. Whatever evaluation one
gives to the work of the Reformers, it cannot be denied
that this was their purpose. Notoriously, their only passion
was to find their way back to the essential kernel. For
this reason it was an actual "re-formation," where the
original, which though hidden and overgrown surely was
present in the Roman church, might come into its own.

The Reformation was a positive movement in its innermost nature, but because it was a purification, took of necessity a negative attitude toward the established order, toward a form of Christianity which undeniably contained great Christian values, but too often hid what was central in the witness of the apostles concerning Christ.

In the last chapter we saw what was essential in the Reformer's understanding of Christianity. Just as there is a very plain relationship between the Roman view of grace and faith and the whole concept of the church as a priestly-sacramental organ of salvation, so there is also a direct line from the Evangelicals' view of these things to their concept of the church and its nature, its means of grace and worship.

What is determinative for Evangelicals is the great and joyous message of God's act in Jesus Christ toward man who, in spite of being created for community with God, is nevertheless in flight from his Creator and Lord. In his love God himself bends down to his created man for the purpose of creating fellowship between himself and the sinner. This is the work of Jesus Christ. Even as he went to sinners and publicans as their brother, so God binds himself to man. In Christ, God truly enters into the life of earthly man, into his battle with all the pernicious powers of sin and death, into the battle against man's pride and his rebellious self, against futility, all bitter suffering and human injustice, in order to save man, to restore his creation. For this reason, "God became man," as stated in the Nicene Creed. According to the Evangelical understanding, this is true in a realistic sense.

It would be impossible to describe what takes place here by speaking of the supernatural infusion of a divine spiritual grace which allies itself with human nature and elevates it to a divine plane whereby men become capable of doing supernatural acts that will give assurance of eternal life.

This supernatural infusion by which spiritual powers are poured into man through the mysteries of sacraments mediated through the ordained priesthood does not exist in Evangelical doctrine. Here a personal word is heard; here something completely personal happens in the holy acts. What does happen? The fallen, sinful, and ego-orientated man, who lives for himself and not in community with God, not in brotherly fellowship with his neighbor, and who is thus under the righteous judgment of the law, now in the midst of his life confronts God, not the condemning God of the law but the merciful and restoring God of grace as he has revealed himself in Jesus Christ.

In this manner a completely new existence is created in which man by God's forgiveness is given a new life in community with him, in the fellowship of the church, and in love toward other men. The curse upon life and the vicious circle is broken, and God's blessing bursts forth. This world's created life can then be lived in faith and joy, in a daily sense of calling to service, in obedience even when God's commands seem to be unreasonable. Life is now to be lived through all sufferings and under that cross which God allows men to carry and through which he breaks down the old ego which in its life of greed is a false realization of man's true and natural destiny as a creation of God. Also in this life man is called to practice love's good works in faith, not with the slightest thought of thereby earning eternal life but because faith cannot do otherwise; and also because that new life is actually in the same breath God's demand upon the entire human life. All this is given in Christ. For this reason everything that takes place in the church, which is the servant of this saving gospel, serves this new life in faith and love, in worship and thanksgiving.

Also, there is an intimate relationship between Christ and his congregation according to the Evangelical view. Christ enters personally into the life of man, not to the single individual apart from the congregation, but in the church and through the external means of grace. Through the word of proclamation and through the sacraments, Christ enters the life of man. Everything in the church is a servant of Christ himself. In his free grace Christ uses these means, not because he is bound to them, but because he binds us to himself with them. According to the Roman Catholic view it is correct to speak of the church as a priestly-sacramental, supernatural organism of salvation. But this is an impossible expression according to Evangelicals, who are not concerned with infusing the divine powers of grace, but with grace conceived as God's free and merciful coming to sinful men.

We must try to be more precise about this. It will have been noticed in the previous discussion that a specific word was constantly used in defining the Evangelical concept of the church that we did not meet in the description of the Roman view. That word is gospel or proclamation. It is peculiar that Thomas Aquinas, for example, in the section of his *Summa* dealing with how salvation is communicated, does not speak of proclamation at all. Only the sacraments are mentioned. And this is consistent with his understanding of salvation. Of course this does not mean that there is no preaching or significance attached to preaching in the Roman church, but it does indicate that the proclamation of the word does not play an essential role as a means of grace. In the great encyclical on the Christian liturgy, *Mediator Dei,* of November 20, 1947, Pope Pius XII mentions preaching last as one of the things that have been instituted for the sanctification of men. But the sermon is defined in a characteristic manner; the preacher shall: 1) Call to mind the laws and commands of the divine Master, 2) Remember the most important circumstances of His life, and 3) Give to the believers appropriate advice and teaching. These viewpoints are not unimportant but, according to the Evangelical conception, that which is decisive is lacking: the proclamation of the good news, the witness to the new event which has taken place.

The New Testament lays an overwhelming weight upon proclamation, both upon what is public and what takes place privately. The biblical word for this preaching, *kerygma,* refers to the herald's proclamation of an important matter. A preacher is not primarily a teacher nor is he one who tells about his own experiences or those of someone else, but he is a messenger whose responsibility it is to shout out that message that he has received. We get an idea of what a preacher is in the account of that messenger who, after the Greeks had defeated the Persians at Marathon, ran the long way back to Athens and there shouted out the tidings of victory to his countrymen and then fell over dead. He did not philosophize about the victory nor did he tell how it was achieved or what impression it made upon him. All this was absolutely secondary in relationship to the great and decisive fact: the victory had been won, and everything had thereby been changed. We preach not ourselves but Christ, says the apostle Paul.

The fact that the gospel is proclaimed is of decisive significance according to the Evangelical conception. The first thing that the apostles did when they received the Spirit on Pentecost was to proclaim the gospel. Accordingly the pronouncement of the word is a means of grace, an instrument of Christ's saving work upon earth. Through the word God confronts man in his conscience and in his innermost personal "I." Through the word, man faces both the judgment of the law and the forgiveness of the gospel. Therefore the proclamation is not a hollow sound nor only a means for purely intellectual understanding of some matter, but the address of God, the expression of his power-filled word which creates something new in man. "For I am not ashamed of the gospel: it is the power of God for salvation to every one who has faith," says Paul (Rom. 1:16). The proclaimed gospel is a dynamic power, a means of revelation of God's will and action. Therefore, proclamation belongs to God's revelatory work down through the ages through which the battle against the powers of corruption and against man's "sacred egoism" constantly continues, and through which the grace of God is constantly extended to mankind.

Through the word, the act of Christ is always alive and real. Not only in a manner that we now know something about it, but in a way that it constantly takes place. We all know the caricature of the proclamation: the eternally preaching preacher. Caricatures can be drawn of both Evangelical and Roman Catholic ministers. And a caricature always contains a very pointed truth. Evangelical churches call themselves the "Church of the Word." How often this has become the "Church of Words!" Between these two there is a vast chasm. The Evangelical church knows best itself where the shoe pinches! But this does not do away with the fact that the word itself operates as a means of grace through which the new world comes into existence here and now. When Luther says that the church is not a "pen house" but a "mouth house," he is referring to the mystery which lies in the hearing of God's word for salvation. It is always a human word—how could it be otherwise—but a human word which the living God takes unto himself and expresses as his own. It is true now as well as in the time of Jesus: He who has ears to hear, let him hear. The word can lie dead upon the lips of men, pale as a corpse; but it can also become the residence of the Spirit and its power, and ignite so that tongues are aflame (Grundtvig).

Therefore the word belongs to the *signs* of the church. It is one of the Reformation's accomplishments that it restored this sign, even placed it at the forefront of all signs of the church. Luther expressed himself very clearly and sharply about this: the gospel is—before Eucharist and Baptism—the only and absolutely sure sign by which the church may be known. In brief: "The entire life and substance of the church lies in God's word. I am not speaking of the written gospel but of the oral, preached word." The external church must proclaim this word. If the gospel is corrupted, the church then corrupts its own roots. For this reason the Reformers had to lay so great a weight upon preserving the purity of the gospel against all corruption.

Does this mean that the sacraments are thereby placed in the lesser light? It neither can nor shall be denied that this has often happened in the history of Protestantism and that this has done great harm to the Evangelical church. Even in our own day church history speaks often about this.

If Roman Catholicism historically often veered toward a one-sided and false sacramentalism, then Protestants fell as often into the opposite ditch, generally with the result that where the sacraments fell into disuse, preaching also became false and lifeless. For proclamation and sacraments belong *inseparably* together. What then is the Evangelical view of the sacraments?

It must first of all be noted that the Reformers limited the number of the sacraments to two: Baptism and Holy Communion. It is true that confession played a decisive role for Luther, largely for the sake of the absolution, in which God's own voice to the sinner is to be heard. In both the Augsburg Confession and Luther's Small Catechism, which with the three ecumenical creeds became the confessional writings of the Danish Evangelical church, confession is placed beside Baptism and Holy Communion. But Luther regarded confession as something intimately related to baptism, as a constant recapitulation. For this reason it cannot be considered a sacrament in itself but is the ever new pronouncement of absolution and forgiveness of sin which a man received in his baptism. For the Roman Catholic, the grace of baptism is not effective for man's entire life. That grace is lost when man falls into sin and only by means of another sacrament can man again enter into the state of grace. From the Evangelical point of view, penance is the constant return to the grace of baptism. However one may look at this, it is at any rate not Luther's desire that confession should receive so poor a fate as it has in the Evangelical church. It should be the responsibility of the Evangelical Lutheran church to strive for a renewal of a genuinely Evangelical understanding of confession.

According to the Reformers, the other Roman Catholic sacraments do not have sufficient basis in the Scriptures. They do not meet the main qualification, that a sacrament should be instituted by Christ himself.

The sacraments are not only symbols, not only pious acts through which the individual or the congregation declares its belongingness to Christ. Nor are they supernatural, mysterious acts which implant the spiritual grace in the soul of man which sanctify and raise men to divinity. They are symbols insofar as a physical act is concerned, with the completely distinct mark of a symbol such as the pouring of the water in Baptism interpreted through the word which is knit into that act. Similarly in the Eucharist—a meal of bread and wine—there is knit into the act a distinct word. A symbol, to be sure! The decisive question remains: what does this symbol contain? Both Baptism and the Eucharist are symbols that are also used by other religions. So far as that goes, it is well-known things that Jesus appropriates, gives to his disciples and, through them, to his church. But the one thing that is all-important is that in Christianity these acts receive a definite content, become the means of a definite act. This content, this act is very simple: Christ himself. He alone is the content of the signs, the functioning power in that which takes place.

The Roman Catholic statement that through the sacraments divine grace is at work—implanted in the human soul —is altogether too weak. Evangelical Christianity asserts that Christ himself comes to men in these symbols inasmuch as he uses these symbols in his sovereign freedom and his mercy as means of his salvatory work in our midst. The content of the sacraments is not a divinely created gift of grace—but Christ himself. Since this is the case, it is also natural that there is only one way in which the sacrament can be received, namely in faith. This simply means, in accord with what we have said earlier, that man receives Christ, not as some achievement whereby he now in some new manner is back in the grip of the law, but rather that when man meets Christ in the act and the word of the sacrament he surrenders completely to the dominion and power of his grace.

This is also true of infant baptism. There it is God's act toward the child even before he is conscious of himself, which he shall receive in faith and thanksgiving as he matures. It is very difficult to attempt to speculate about what occurs when men receive the sacraments in any other manner than in faith, understood as the personally receptive and obedient relationship to Christ. In speculation, everything becomes confused, because sacraments and faith belong together even as Christ and faith belong together. Without faith Christ does not cease to be Christ, but man's relationship to him has then become something completely different. But one very significant thing must be added to this—it is not we who are to decide when there is faith or no faith—but God alone. God here also has the power and the sovereignty which sees and understands all, and therefore he alone may judge.

Into God's created but fallen world Christ has come, Savior and Lord. He is the prophet who speaks the word of truth, the king who rules and establishes his kingdom and restores the good order of the creation in the midst of the chaos of sin and death, and the priest who, as a substitute, bears the sin of the people. Christ is, as Origen so beautifully expressed it, *autobasileia*, God's kingdom himself. He is the coming kingdom of God present now in the midst of us on this old earth. God's kingdom has already broken through in him. As the risen and ascended Lord, he is constantly in the midst of his people. The kingdom has not yet come in its glory and its fulness, but it continually breaks through all the obstacles of sin and death. It is a present power pointing toward that moment when the kingdom itself will break through in the event which we call the second coming of Christ.

To be in community with this prophet, king, and high priest is to know eternal life already here on earth. It is this to which the herald invites in the proclamation and which he proclaims as the great incomprehensible reality. It is for this that Baptism and Holy Communion, confession and absolution are Christ's own means. Hidden in the signs but thereby no less present, Christ constantly fulfils his work. Through these signs he builds his new people and his new world, often in great and painful secrecy and obscurity but nevertheless as a reality.

The sacraments are the "place" where the coming kingdom of God again and again breaks into the old world. They are the place where man is confronted by his real destiny, not in the proclamation of a consuming judgment, not in a religious philosophy nor in the mystical workings of a mysterious religion, but in a living person, Christ himself. He comes constantly to us in a bodily form, in a saving word, in a very simple and natural act which by his word has become the means of his saving power. To the question of why Jesus has chosen such external tangible means, which seem to suit the so-called modern man so poorly, one can only answer that he has so ordained it and that his church has faithfully retained this. But the manner in which these means are understood is important, and it is here that the battle rages. They receive their meaning from the view which the church has toward the work of Christ and the relationship between God and man. It is this entire view which is different within Roman and Evangelical Christianity. For this reason there will also be a decisive difference in the use of "the goods of the church."

Both the proclamation of the word and the administration of the sacraments, according to the Evangelical conception, can be performed by ordinary men. Evangelicals regard the idea that administration of the sacraments requires some special spiritual equipment as a false understanding of the Christian ministry. For example it would be absolutely impossible for an Evangelical Christian to concede the following words of the pastoral letter of the Cardinal of Salzburg written in 1905 in which he speaks of the office of the Roman priest in the administration of the sacrament of the altar: "Where in heaven or on earth is there power like that which a Catholic priest possesses? Mary gave birth to the divine child for this earth but once, and look, the priest does this not once but hundreds and thousands of times, as often as he celebrates the mass . . . Christ has given to the priests power over His holy humanity; even, as it were, given them power over His Body. The Catholic priest cannot only make Jesus present upon the altar but can shut Him up in the tabernacle, and again take Him out and give Him to the believers so they may partake of Him. Christ the only born Son of the Father through whom heaven and earth have been created obeys him in this action."

More officially this same view is repeated in Pius XI's encyclical concerning the Roman priesthood (*Ad Catholici*

Sacerdotii of December 20, 1935) wherein the Pope states that the inexpressible greatness of the priest is shown in all its glory in the fact that he possesses the power over the body of Jesus Christ and makes this immanent upon our altars. In the very tone of voice and choice of words as well as in the viewpoint itself there is something here that is foreign and often offensive to the Evangelical consciousness.

This does not mean that Evangelical Lutheran Christianity does not recognize the office of the ministry within the church. Evangelical Christians acknowledge with thankfulness that service in the congregation which God has given to particular men. The Reformers are not in doubt about this for one moment, nor is there doubt in the confessional writings of Lutheranism. It is stated very clearly in the Augsburg Confession that God has instituted the office of the ministry of the gospel, i.e., ministry for Christ in his saving work down through all ages. This is the ministry of the proclamation of the gospel and the administration of the holy sacraments. It is an office which is understood as an indispensable part of the congregation, an office instituted by Christ and his apostles, through which the church is built up as the body of Christ. As an aid to the body of Christ in fulfilling its service here on earth, Christ has given to the church the various offices as they are described in chapter four of the letter to the Ephesians.

Accordingly it is faulty, in the opinion of the Reformers, to say that the ministry has been established only for "the sake of order." If one thereby maintains that everything that has to do with the office or with that particular service is in reality something completely subordinate, which the congregation has introduced for purely practical and therefore also unessential reasons, which it also has full freedom to abolish again if this should prove to be even more practical, then this is an absolute contradiction of the genuinely Evangelical Lutheran point of view. Many are afraid that the office shall establish a ruling hierarchy in the church and create an intermediary position between God and man. To put it briefly, they are afraid of the Roman Catholic point of view. The reply must be that, according to the Evangelical conception, the office never can create such an "intermediary position" between God and man any more than it constitutes a special class of men provided with spiritual powers that exceed what all the other members of the church have. The minister is not something "special" with an indelible character that he has received through a sacrament of ordination. The office is a *service* in the midst of the congregation, not in any way above the congregation. It is a service which belongs to the entire congregation and is entrusted by it to certain men. It exists for the sake of the congregation and serves to protect the congregation from self-appointed authority of an individualistic character and perhaps thereby a rather "tyrannic" influence.

In ordination this ministry that was instituted by Christ is assigned to them that know themselves called to it and who request that they may participate therein. This assignment takes place by prayer and the laying on of hands as a visible sign that this person has now accepted this distinct service which is given to him and not to all the others and under whose blessing and responsibility he is now to live. It is this view of the ministry which received clear and beautiful expression at the synod at Barmen in 1934, which said: "The various offices of the Church do not give grounds for any lordship of one part over any other but are the exercise of that service which is given as a command and entrusted to the entire congregation."

Through ordination the minister receives in a visible manner a share in the ministry to proclaim the gospel, to administer the holy sacraments, and to pronounce the words of absolution. He has no indelible character, but is simply an ordinary Christian who is delegated and entrusted with a special service. In this office, he is the servant of the congregation—not that he personally is dependent upon the congregation and must please it in the exercise of his service, but rather that he is to serve it with that message and with those goods which God has given to his church.

We note, for example, that Melanchthon puts a very high estimate upon ordination, and even has nothing against considering it a sacrament. But he energetically opposes the viewpoint which sees the minister as a man with special powers to transform the elements of the Eucharist and to present an offering. The minister is not a sacrificial priest, but one who has been delegated to proclaim the word and distribute the sacrament. In that service, he does not have any unique "power and authority" *in himself,* but all authority remains in the word of God. It is God himself who in his free grace makes use of human means to establish his sovereignty upon the earth. On this question the view of the Evangelical Reformation is often found walking a narrow line between seeking to divorce itself clearly from the Roman Catholic concepts of the priestly office and at the same time maintaining the importance of that special office as something necessary and given by Christ himself as witnessed to in both the New Testament and in the Lutheran confessional writings.

Both Evangelicals and Romans agree that the worship service contains an inner as well as an external factor. In the history of the church we meet time and again that well-known phenomenon, common in the history of religion, of the external element completely overshadowing the inner. The correctly conducted ritual or ceremony becomes dominating so that worship becomes an external cultus or simply ends in that caricature of true worship—magic. At the same time the relationship to God becomes mechanical and men develop a static form of religion, a type of *theurgi,* in which man in the cult has the power over God. No part of the church has completely escaped this danger.

But we also know the exact opposite. Out of sheer fear of the externals, fear of the form or the rigidity of the worship service, men have believed that the less form there was, the more content, the more spirit, there would be. If not directly harmful, the external form was nevertheless considered absolutely unimportant. God does not meet man through the externals but through the inward experiences, through an inner light or in a mystical quietness. The worship service—if on the whole it could be called that—became a completely subjective, individualistic, and spiritualistic religiosity without any external, "bodily" expression of the relationship to God.

Without seeking to generalize, one can probably say that the danger of the externally, ritualistically defined cult form where the weight to an overwhelming degree, is laid upon the external element or the correctly performed action has been, and is greater within Catholicism—both in the Greek Orthodox and in the Roman churches. One needs only to read the so-called *rubricae*, so named because of the red print in the Roman book of the mass, in order to see the degree to which external regulations of ritual determine the nature of the worship and obligate the officiating priest. The external form of the mass is defined to the very finest detail. Roman Catholics themselves acknowledge that there is here a possibility of real derailment of a true and valid worship.

In the same manner, the opposite danger, which views worship in terms of pure "spirituality" is greatest within Protestantism. In the attempt, often made in justifiable eagerness, to establish "pure worship" by rooting out the external forms, it is noteworthy that the content for which the forms were only supposed to be the frame slipped completely through the fingers. Content will always demand its form, and spirit will always demand a body in which to live. No person here on earth lives in pure spirituality. It is not rare within Protestantism to have lost worthwhile elements, some of them very old, because their value for worship and for faith was not appreciated.

However there is in principle a certain agreement between the Roman and the Evangelical Lutheran understanding of worship in the fact that both—as has been mentioned—acknowledge both an inner and an external factor of the worship service. The Roman church knows that the most vital element of the liturgy is the inner reality. Otherwise religion becomes an empty ceremony and sheer formalism. This is very forcefully stated by Pope Pius XII in his great encyclical on the Christian Liturgy, 1947, which is also highly worth reading and studying by Protestants.

And in a newly published book about the mass, the

preface reads: "There is no difference of opinion concerning this, that the inward factor has decisive precedence in prayer. Without the inward life, there is no outward worship. The Christian shepherd of souls must in reality have been abandoned by all good spirits and have completely perverted the intentions of Christ if he thinks he can honor God *with lips alone* or with a purely aesthetic form of symbolical actions." The red print in the book of the mass, the directions for the liturgist, is always second to the black print, the text of the worship service.

On the whole, the powerful liturgical movement in the Roman church reflects not only the desire for a worthily conducted worship service, but far more the desire to make the content of the service come alive for the believers so that they truly participate in the liturgical life of the church. The service of worship is seen here in the light of profound fervor.

At the same time, there is a movement taking place in the Evangelical Lutheran church to clarify the fact that worship also has its externals and that the so-called pure and "spiritual" worship service with its contempt and indifference toward the external factors very easily becomes a hollowed-out, subjective worship service. Moreover, its formlessness is also a kind of "form." Luther's own views on these matters are instructive for Evangelical Christians. He observes that freedom from forms belongs to heaven—not to earth. That which he energetically and even with violence opposed whenever talk turned to form and content was the opinion that some external form should be considered sacrosanct and untouchable, divinely commanded and arranged. In connection with this he recalled with horror the Roman mass with all its minute rubrics of purely

ritualistic nature. Luther considered it blasphemous that
the form should be regarded holy and untouchable to that
degree.

The form is not unimportant but neither is it divine. No
external orders can make the claim of being an absolute
in the relationship between God and man. Where the
gospel is rightly proclaimed and the sacraments are administered in accord with the Scriptures, i.e., in agreement
with the words of institution, there can be found the true
worship service. But this worship service does have its
form, and here Luther showed himself to be conservative.
He proceeded from the traditional worship service and did
not attempt to create a completely new liturgy. He had
an understanding of the church and of history. He sought
to cleanse it from those ingredients which the Reformers
believed were in conflict with the gospel of God's great
glory and grace. "I do not condemn any external ceremonies," he wrote in a letter to a pastor in Kiel in 1528,
"except those which are in conflict with the Gospel."
And he heartily disassociated himself from those people
who, out of their own religious fantasy, tried to shape new
worship services with new, free, and ingenious liturgies.
The external form is necessary, not for the sake of God but
for the sake of man, as a means to serve the cause itself,
although it is never synonymous with it. Or, to express this
even more strongly: the innermost intent of the worship
service is to serve as the means of Christ's living presence
with his people.

We have thus arrived at the heart of the matter: in the
worship service something takes place. We have seen in
our study so far a strong tension between Romans and
Evangelicals concerning worship, although their relation-

ship also contains a certain agreement. In understanding the content of worship, both contradictions and similarities become evident. But again, this contrast has as its background a common point of departure: the worship service as Christ's living presence with his people.

In the Roman Catholic interpretation, the Mass is "truly and properly the offering of a sacrifice." Christ here again through the hands of the priest and in fellowship with the whole of his mystical body offers himself anew to the heavenly Father. Hardly anywhere does the significance of the ordained priesthood show itself as great as at this point. Through his ordination the priest has in a unique degree received an equality with the High Priest and is enabled to act in Christ's own power and to perform in his name. The sacrifice of the Mass is spoken of as a "representation" of the sacrifice of Christ upon the cross. The sacrifice of the Mass is the same act that took place upon the cross when Jesus offered himself in his real earthly body, in part to render true glory, honor, and thanksgiving to God, and in part to accomplish expiation and atonement. Christ offers himself thousands of times upon the altar, both for the living and the dead. As a matter of fact a great number of the masses that are read are "soul masses" for the dead in purgatory.

From the priest's opening prayer at the foot of the altar, through the *Kyrie,* the *Gloria,* and the so-called "pre-Mass" where the *Word* (scripture reading, prayer, hymns, and confession of faith) is the essential, to the actual "sacrificial-Mass" (the presentation of sacrificial gifts and the "canon" of the Mass, the kernel of this sacred ceremony) everything in the liturgy aims toward that moment when the priest silently voices the words of consecration over the

bread and the wine through which transubstantiation takes
place. From this very moment Christ is present upon the
altar in the "condition of the sacrifice" (*in statu victimae*).
The consecrated host is "reserved" and is made the object
of worship also outside the mass itself.

The sacrifice of the Mass has been the object of very
detailed discussions, not least in modern time. But it is not
this side of the matter which concerns the ordinary believer. For him the mysterious moment of the transformation is the main concern, the presence of Christ in the transformed elements.

What role does the congregation itself play in this? It is
strongly urged to participate personally in the ceremony
of the Mass and not to pray just its own private prayers or
simply consider it all as a dramatic performance. In the
encyclical concerning the liturgy, Pope Pius XII strongly
underscores that the congregation shall participate in the
act of sacrifice by becoming one in that spiritual attitude of
praise, prayer, and expiation which governs the priest, even
Christ himself. They are to transform themselves and rid
themselves of all sin so that they, "together with the immaculate Host of the sacrifice will become an acceptable
oblation to the eternal Father." The believers become one
with Christ in the Mass, not only in the acts of sacrifice
itself but also by offering themselves.

The sermon plays a subordinate role in this constantly
renewed service of sacrifice. The epistle and the gospel
are regarded as the proclamation part of the Mass. A place
for a sermon can be found but it is not necessary or common. As already mentioned, the entire understanding of
the oral, proclaimed word is different than it is for Evangelicals. For this reason there will always be a distinct

contrast in the way the word is preached in the two churches.

But the Mass is more than an offering, *sacrificium*. It is also a sacrament, Holy Communion. The sacrifice is knit into the common meal which gives to the believer the heavenly bread, the body of Jesus Christ, which unites man with Christ and constitutes an increase of divine grace in the soul. As a sacrament, Holy Communion is the feast of spiritual food by which the soul is nurtured and strengthened. It also serves as an antidote to free man from the daily forgivable sins and to preserve man against the mortal sins. Mortal sins are not forgiven in Holy Communion. Just the opposite: it is a condition for a worthy and valid participation in this sacrament that these have already been forgiven through the sacrament of penance. "That one who says that the most important fruit of the holy Eucharist is the forgiveness of sin, or that this is the only work of the Holy Communion, let him be excommunicated," says the Council of Trent. According to the Roman Catholic interpretation, the most important effect of Holy Communion is the increase of that grace which already exists in the soul.

A congregation is not absolutely necessary for the act of the Mass or the celebration of the Eucharist. It is sufficient that the priest himself reads the Mass together with his assistant, and that he partakes of the transformed elements. It is well-known that laymen only receive the one element of the sacrament. This restriction, which probably roots originally in the fear of the laymen that they might spill some of the wine that had been changed into the blood of Christ, was strongly attacked by the Reformers who regarded it a misuse of the Eucharist.

Allow this scanty presentation to be sufficient to give an impression of the Roman Mass. And let us for a moment consider the Evangelical interpretation of the Mass, a name which, incidentally, is also used in the Scandinavian Evangelical churches.

The Evangelical churches also regard worship as communion with God. It is not primarily a meeting for edification but one held in the presence of God. The worship service is the face-to-face meeting of the Triune God in God's saving act of revelation with his congregation upon the earth. Because of this the Evangelical service of worship cannot be imagined without a congregation who share this worship together. The word which is spoken and proclaimed demands someone to whom it is to be spoken and for whom it is to be proclaimed. For this reason it must be conducted in the mother tongue, understandable by all. It should be stressed that what takes place does not happen only up at the altar in the chancel of the church but in the midst of the gathering of the congregation. Therefore the priest and the congregation can never do two different things but they are bound together in one and the same action. The worship service is from its very basis congregational worship.

What takes place there? The living Christ is present with his salvation. There is to be heard God's law which embraces the entire life of man and before which man stands guilty, and the gospel of God, that ever new and incomprehensible message concerning forgiveness and freedom. This proclamation of the good news is an indispensable component of Evangelical worship in its main form. It is the public word, a voice which shall be sounded far and wide. It is not a stereotyped repetition, but a proclamation which is continuously directed toward each particular time and people. It is the proclamation of Christ as Lord and Savior, he who forgives and receives the entirety of human life under his Lordship.

The message is heard too in the words of the Apostles' Creed, in the hymns, in the reading of Scripture. And the congregation answers in its own confession of sin and guilt, in its confession of faith, and in its praise and thanksgiving. From the depths are heard the songs of praise for that salvation in which the children of the earth may share.

In immediate connection with prayer, confession, hymns, and sermon, follows the celebration of Holy Communion. At this very point the main division between the Roman Catholics and the Evangelical Lutherans has existed since the time of the Reformation. According to the Evangelical position there can be no talk of a "sacrificial mass" as Roman Catholic theology understands it. Christ died one time for all, the sacrifice was made one time for all. In the Holy Communion the sacrifice of Jesus made once for all is present in the congregation. A direct line goes back from every celebration of Holy Communion to the cross of Jesus Christ, which alone gives life to the world. We approach here the innermost reality of Christianity. Time stands still in the sacrament of the Eucharist, and the congregation gathers itself about the crucified and risen Lord, who is truly present to give to his people a participation in his atonement and resurrection. But in the Evangelical view there is no "sacrifice," either as a "repetition" or as a "representation." Therefore the minister is not a sacrificial priest nor is the altar table a place of sacrifice. At that table Christ himself celebrates Holy Communion with his people, by giving his body and blood to sinful men and making them partakers of his eternal sacrifice.

Evangelical Lutheran faith holds the concept which the theologians call "the real presence," which means that Christ is truly present in the celebration of the sacrament in the bread and wine, solely by the power of the word of Christ's own institution, which is the focal point in every Holy Communion.

Holy Communion is an "act of God's kingdom" in which the coming kingdom of God breaks through now to our earthly existence, with all the gifts of that kingdom. The first and foremost gift is Christ, who is himself the kingdom, *autobasileia,* as has been mentioned. The Sacrament of the Altar is "the bread of the pilgrims on their journey," *cibus viatorum,* which derives all its power from Christ, the crucified and risen, and which points forward to the coming meal of glory in God's kingdom where Christ will be visibly and gloriously present. It is the meal of the church here on earth midway between the meal of Holy Thursday and the meal in the coming kingdom of God. For this reason this sacrament is the Eucharist, which means that it is a feast of thanksgiving where praise ever breaks forth anew about what has taken place in Christ. Holy Communion is a meal of joy because life, blessedness, and the forgiveness of sins are to be found where Christ himself is. Man receives his life back from God anew. He receives everything in faith. And through that faith God re-establishes his fallen creation.

The Sacrament of the Altar is likewise the meal of fellowship where Christ shares the meal with completely ordinary earthly men even as he gathered with tax collectors and sinners during his earthly life to the offense of the Phari-

sees who considered such a fellowship absolutely intoler-
able and scandalous. The only ones that are excluded are
those who exclude themselves because they consider themselves too good and too pious to be found there in solidarity
with other earthly and sinful men.

There are not many who have so strongly described
Holy Communion in terms of fellowship as did Luther.
In one of his writings concerning the sacrament he names
it specifically the sacrament of fellowship—*communio*.

This fellowship has a double nature. In the first place,
it is fellowship between Christ and sinful, worldly men in
distress. This community is absolute. Christ enters *completely* into the life of man and does not consider himself
too good to share everything with us, including poverty,
temptation, spiritual distress, and all evil. Therefore no
Christian is ever alone, but is always embraced by the fellowship of the saints. If he suffers evil or is tempted by
grievous sins, he may go in frankness to the table of the
Lord, because there he will meet Christ, who became man
completely and fully. But he shall then also know that
here we are speaking of another fellowship as well, the
fellowship mutually shared by men. Just as Christ became
our neighbor and "transformed" himself to our state and
took everything that is ours upon himself, so shall we
also live together with our neighbor and share conditions
with him. For this reason there is a fellowship here, a
communism if one will, that goes to the very bottom of
things. Here men are united in a fellowship where he who
has much shall share with him who has little. He who has
glory is to share with him who has no glory. He who has
wealth shall share with his poor neighbor. He who is
strong in the resistance of temptation shall come to the

assistance of the one who easily falls—and so on, to the very last facet of the human life. This takes place in love. Therefore this sacrament is the "sacrament of love"—"We become part of each other through love," says Luther. Here Christ transforms himself to us and becomes one with us in all things. In this way Holy Communion is also the model of and the reference to the new humanity which shall become visible and realized when the kingdom is established in God's hour.

From this it can also be understood that the Eucharist is the meal by which the congregation as the body of Christ is built up, and by which the fellowship described in the first chapter is initially being established here on earth. For this reason there is no other place where the "impossibility" of the division is so glaringly obvious, that this table which carries the entire fellowship has become the place of division where one church cuts itself off from the other. The entire problem of "intercommunion," that is, the question of the possibility that members from various churches can meet at each other's communion tables, is in itself the most powerful witness concerning the condition of Christ's church here on earth, where something that is utterly essential has been lost.

It would be wrong and very ungrateful not to indicate that there is also a common "yes" between Roman Catholics and Evangelical Lutherans in regard to this question of the worship service. There are even signs of a growing mutual understanding, not least because of the fellowship of research in the New Testament area. However it is perfectly clear to everyone that, at this very point, the difference becomes tangible because the two churches must each conduct their own worship services with no possibility of being able to meet at the same communion table. Not only the form of the worship service but also its content and fundamental motivation, its understanding of the relationship between God and man, is too different.

The two churches must bear this separation, but they do not have the right to accept it matter-of-factly as something natural and normal. It is actually screamingly not normal. That "no" which is erected here as a wall between them must early and late be cause for repentance and a renewed eagerness to seek their common "yes": the confession of the living Lord and his presence in the worship of the church. In that worship the decisive thing can never be what we do or accomplish but what Christ speaks and works. In the midst of the "no," there *is* a "yes."

Chapter 7

THE SAINTS AND VIRGIN MARY

Before turning to the main subject of this section—
the Roman and the Evangelical view of the Virgin Mary—
it may be appropriate to consider very briefly the problem
of the saints, a question often dealt with in contemporary
literature. In this connection we will not examine the way
literature treats this problem, however interesting that
might be, but confine ourselves to certain theological and
dogmatic definitions in order to understand Roman Catholicism on this point.

What is a saint? A person who is permeated with holiness, with grace, with love. A person in whom grace has
done its sanctifying work in rich measure. As a piece of
iron is permeated with fire, in the same manner a human
soul is permeated by divine grace. It is possible, even
likely, that the person concerned feels this subjectively to
be completely otherwise, as the life of a saint is often a life
of torment, of suffering, and of anonymity, but this changes
nothing of the principal definition.

Roman teaching adds a further consideration. The person who allows himself to be led fully on the way of grace
becomes able to do more than he is obligated to do. Every
person, as a creation of God and as a believer, is obligated
to follow the divine commandments. But it is possible for

a person with the help of grace to go further and to follow the evangelical counsel, which is not the obligation of all but which indicates the way for those who progress further in holiness. For example, by giving up marriage or property or command over one's own self, a person walks on a road where it is possible to do more than one is obligated to do and thereby also to earn more than one personally can use.

Furthermore the church maintains, as we earlier considered in our discussion of indulgences, that this which such a sanctified person does over and above the inescapable measure of obligation, really is something in "excess" which can be of benefit to others. The saints only have this "excess" in relation with and subordinate to the merits of Christ, but together with Christ and under him these earnings form a sort of "holy family estate" which belongs to the church as the mystical body of Christ and which can be distributed by it to other members of the church wherever there is need for it.

Another unique matter concerns the further thought that the church has the right through the so-called canonization process to name certain persons saints. After a process that is often minute and always thorough, the pope can by virtue of his infallibility and therefore with unchallengeable authority undertake the act of canonization. By power of this act a person is declared to have had such a measure of holiness in his life that he may be named among the saints with the right to be invoked by the entire church, to be named in the Mass, to have churches, chapels, and altars dedicated in his name. His or her relics may be preserved, venerated, and displayed for public glorification.

The saints must be venerated but not worshiped. They

may be invoked and their help may be called upon in particular circumstances. They make intercessory prayers for us before God. Hence they come to play a certain middle role between God and man. There is no talk of making an idol of a creation, but nevertheless the created comes to play a significant role in man's relationship with God. Innocent XI in 1687 condemned the following statement of Michael Molinos: "No creation, either of the Blessed Virgin or of the saints ought to have a place in our hearts, for God alone wants to occupy and own that." The Council of Trent has authoritatively determined the relationship to the persons of the saints as well as to their relics and images. This defends explicitly the veneration of the relics and of those things with which a saint has been in contact, as well as of their images. The honoring of such things may not be rejected, for through these a person receives help from the saints.

The main viewpoint is this: the saints cannot save us, for that is God's work alone, but in many respects they can help persons along the way to salvation, since by virtue of the power of their closer relationship to God they can render us help on our pilgrim's way not only in our religious but also in our common earthly life. "God can of course help man without the Saints, but He wills not to help us without their cooperation, because both his nature and his will are communicable love. God saves men in such a manner that all the powers of love in the body of Christ have their share therein" (Karl Adam). In the veneration of the saints by men and in the manifold help given to man by the saints, the Roman Catholic church sees an essential feature of the phrase in the Apostles' Creed, "the communion of saints." The divine blessing never works round-about but always through the unity of the members.

It will be clear from this brief presentation that there is a close relationship between this view and Roman Cathol-icism's entire view of grace and of the church. Grace is the infusion of supernatural power which sanctifies men and steadily increases grace and holiness in the believer. The church is the divine means of salvation with the power and ability to distribute the sanctifying powers and to administer with authority the large "treasury of merits" which spans not only mankind here on earth but also the dead in purgatory and the sainted in heaven.

As strange as it may seem to many, there are points in these ways of thinking that are also indispensable and es-sential to Evangelical Christianity. I am thinking primarily of that fellowship between all Christians in which one may be of aid to another. Here there is constantly found that "communication of benefits" of which Thomas speaks. Evan-gelical Christianity of course also recognizes the fact that God uses men in his service. God has, says Luther, his co-operators, his fellow-workers, both in the orders of crea-tion and redemption. God works through the created, not as some arbitrary impulsive *Deus ex machina*. In the fore-going section on the Eucharist, we indicated some of Luther's thoughts in this matter. There are points where it would be rewarding if Roman and Evangelical Chris-tians would enter into an open conversation in a thorough and objective manner. Here also a common ground will become obvious while at the same time a constantly recur-ring "no" will make itself evident.

What is it in this development so far which conflicts with Evangelical thought? First, the thought that a person can do more than he is obligated to do. The idea of a surplus of good deeds finds no home in Evangelical thought. Even where a person renders that which is exceptional, he is still a poor servant. Luke (17:10) uses the paradoxical expression: an "unworthy servant," who has only done what he was required to do. Man as a creature is completely subject to God. God knows his creation and its condition and knows also the deep differences between men. Therefore he is also his creation's merciful and longsuffering God. But the thought that a person through his life and works, even with the supernatural help of grace, should be able to do more than God in and for himself can demand of him, according to the Evangelical viewpoint, lead to a strangely quantitative and neutral conception of man in which the relationship to God seems to be measured and parceled out.

Even the best and most unselfish person always stands as a debtor before God. He knows himself to be an unworthy servant. No one can come along afterward and change this self-knowledge. If anyone does such a thing it places the good man in a false relationship to God and also to his fellow men.

The good person would be tempted to regard himself as something other than the "unworthy servant" and the fellow men would be tempted to consider him as a kind of superman who has established some priority in relationship to God, or has even become a mediating helper before God. This offers a real danger to the purity and directness of the God-man relationship, a devious way that seems human and "safe," but which is not based upon the Christian revelation.

We are now at the second point where Evangelical

Christendom stands in opposition to the Roman. There is a great difference between believing that God uses others in his service to the individual person, such as God in his wisdom does do, and believing that particular persons stand peculiarly close to God, and that it is therefore good to call upon them to help us by interceding for us with God. In this sense, Evangelical Christianity does not accept people who are go-betweens between God and people here on earth. The fellowship and inherent dependency between men is not denied, but it is to be emphasized as something unmistakable in Christianity that the individual confronts God directly.

To believe on Jesus Christ is to be placed in a completely new relationship to God who in Jesus' name is the Father of man. This name, which is the name Jesus applied to God, means that there is complete openness and free access to God, to whom no one is a stranger. In this father-child relationship to God, everything is given. As human beings during Jesus' earthly life could go directly to him, man can now also, without any mediary, go directly to him, assured that he hears their prayers. It is none of man's concern to meddle in the question of how God helps him. The child leaves this to his heavenly Father in complete confidence. It is therefore impossible for the Evangelical Christian to accept any part of Karl Adam's very categorical statement: "God *can* of course help us without the saints, but he *will* not help us without their cooperation."

Only one thing is determinative for us: that in Christ there is direct access for every person to the Father in heaven. To allow something else to intrude, or what is worse, to put it into the church's teaching as has happened in the cultus and piety of the Roman Catholic church, will always be a stumbling block for Evangelical Christendom.

Here we come to the third point. Evangelical Christianity cannot recognize the right of the church to determine through a canonization process and proclamation that certain people are saints and thereby receive a privileged standing in the relationship between God and men. In the first place, a basic misunderstanding of holiness is found here with which the Evangelical view cannot be reconciled. In addition, according to the Evangelical concept, this is based upon a mistaken understanding of the church. The church has no right to canonize and has no treasure of surplus good deeds which it can dispense. According to the Evangelical concept, the church's task is one single thing: under all circumstances to lead men to God himself, to Jesus Christ himself, who is a living reality in his word and in his sacraments. To want to do other things—perhaps more than this—results in doing less.

Now at this point the Roman church would say this is exactly what it wants to do: to make Christ the *only* mediator between God and man. Evangelical Christendom considers this obscured by the Roman Catholic church's great emphasis on the saints in both teaching and cultus. It is true that in Roman Catholicism the Christian life is given a tinge of humanness and "intelligibility," and also at times of simple logic. But this cannot draw Evangelical Christianity away from the biblical apostolic message that all is given in Jesus Christ in whom men have free and unhindered access to the Father, certain that he before whose eye all life is spread hears prayers and knows how and by what means he shall help his children. Therefore, Evangelical Christians do not call upon the saints as their particular helpers. This does not exclude there being men who strengthen the faith because we see through their lives how they themselves have shared in God's grace and have lived their lives therein. But this is something that belongs to a completely different realm than the Roman Catholic teaching about saints.

We shall now try to clarify for our own understanding that person who, after the triune God, plays the greatest role in Roman Christianity—the Virgin Mary. In the great host of saints she has an unconditional first place; in fact, her place in the relationship between God and man cannot in reality be compared to that of any other saint.

It is not easy to write about the Virgin Mary because Evangelical Christianity at this point very easily misunderstands Roman thought. On the other hand, Mariolatry has taken constantly richer forms through the centuries, even as Mariology, the true teaching of the church about the mother of the Lord, has become steadily clearer through the great dogmatic definitions and through numerous papal encyclicals of the past century.

The following material refrains from considering what one might call the Mary worship of the folkways and is restricted to the teachings of the Roman Catholic church. The basis for all genuine Roman veneration of Mary is Mary as the mother of Jesus. In a way everything beyond this which is said, taught, and believed about Mary in the Roman church is secondary, or ought to become so, as Mary is only someone in relationship with another and this other is her Son, Jesus Christ. It is for his sake and only by virtue of his power that Mary is anything at all. "The glories of Mary are for the sake of her son," said Cardinal Newman.

First, a bit of history. In the New Testament and in the post-apostolic times, Mary plays no particular role. However, she is named by Ignatius, Justin, Irenaeus, and Tertullian, by whom a particular parallel between Eve and Mary is presented. As Eve brought misfortune upon man through her disobedience, Mary, with her obedience, corrected the fault of the first Eve. The antithesis of Mary and Eve corresponds to the antithesis of Christ and Adam. A significant turning point takes place at the great church meeting at Ephesus in 431. It was here that the expression, "God's mother" or more correctly, the one who gave birth to God, *Theotokos*, came forth.

It was not so much to emphasize something about the Virgin Mary as about Christ that this expression became used, because it had to be emphasized that Jesus *was* truly God's only begotten Son. Mary had not only given birth to a great person but truly to God's Son, the divine second person of the Trinity. For this reason it was not enough to call Mary the mother of Christ, but necessary to call her the mother of God. The same One who is born of the Father in eternity is conceived and born of the Virgin Mary. Her Son is that One through whom the world is created.

From this point on, worship of Mary, as well as Mariology, gathers momentum. Churches were dedicated to Mary, pictures of her were honored, festivals in praise and remembrance of her were introduced into the liturgy. The four oldest are the festival of Mary's birth, (September 8); purification (February 2); annunciation (March 25); and her ascension (August 15). Through Ephraim Syrer (d. 373) the Mary poetry was begun; and both by Augustine and even more by the fathers of the following centuries ending with John of Damascus (d. 749), the teachings concerning Mary developed hand in hand with the growing veneration of Mary. In the seventh and eighth centuries there was hardly a town that did not have a church dedicated to Mary.

The Middle Ages saw the flowering of worship of the Virgin Mary. A special Mariology developed, favored by the greatest theologians of the Middle Ages such as Bernard of Clairvaux, Albert the Great, Bonaventura, Thomas Aquinas, and many more, and at the same time the poetry about Mary reached its pinnacle. From the eleventh century stems the most beloved of the hymns to Mary, "Salve Regina," and since the fourteenth century the famous sequence, "Stabat Mater Dolorosa" has been sung, which now has its place in both the feasts of Mary's seven sorrows as well as among the hymns in the breviary. From the Middle Ages also comes "Ave Maria," the angelic greeting to Mary, the most exalted and beloved prayer to God's mother in western Catholicism. Together with the Lord's Prayer, this forms the introduction to every canonical hour, and is the essential component of the Rosary, which according to legend was given to the holy Dominicus by the Virgin Mary herself as the best guard against heresy. At the conclusion of the Middle Ages, the feast of the Holy Rosary was set (October 7).

Under Pius IX, the veneration of Mary reached a new height through the "Dogma of Mary's Immaculate Conception," December 8, 1854. In 1858 Mary revelations occurred at Lourdes which with Fatima in Portugal became the most famous places of pilgrimage. Other places of pilgrimage are Loretto, Kevelaer, Einsiedeln and Guadalupe. The existing Mary congregations, which were already numerous, grew in number and new Mary festivals were named, for example, to Mary's immaculate heart (August 22), and to Mary as the means of all grace (May 31). Well known are the Mary encyclicals of Leo XIII which year after year urged prayer to Mary, especially the prayer of the Rosary. In 1942, Pope Pius XII invoked the entire world in prayer to the heart of Mary that she might intercede with God for more peaceful times for the church and for humanity. In the bull, *Munificentissimus Deus*, Pope Pius XII proclaimed on November 1, 1950, the "Dogma of Mary's Assumption," thereby fulfilling a century-old burning wish of Roman Catholic people. With the exception of the Middle Ages there has hardly been a time in the history of the Roman church which has been so preoccupied with Mary as our own time has been. Not only the folk-piety, but also learned scholarship, the flowering Mary literature, pictorial art, and liturgy's new developments, have vied with each other in praising the mother of God and the queen of heaven.

The principle features in the Roman Catholic veneration of Mary are the following:

1. *The privileges of Mary.* In the course of time, the Virgin Mary has been given various "privileges," as they are termed in Roman Catholic theological language. These are fitting and proper for the mother of God, whom God from eternity has set aside to be the mother of his Son and therefore loved with a love that surpasses his love of every other creation.

The first of these privileges is her virginity, not only in the understanding given us in the Apostles' Creed, that Jesus received his existence through a direct act of creation by God, but in such a way that Mary is a virgin before the birth of Jesus, in the birth, and after the birth (*virgo ante partum, in partu,* and *post partum*). There was a miracle also in the birth itself, for Jesus was born without any damage whatsoever being done to her virginity. Even as God's word in his eternal birth does not disturb anything in the nature of the triune God, even as he as the risen One passed through closed doors, so Jesus was born, without any damage to Mary's holy womb. Although not based upon any historic communication, it was fitting for the Son of God to enter the world in such a way. He who had come to heal could not destroy; he who commanded us to love our fathers and mothers could not by his birth rob his mother of so high a privilege.

And as Mary was a virgin in the birth, she remained a virgin throughout her life. She had perpetual virginity. When Jesus' brothers and sisters are mentioned, these are not words concerning brothers and sisters of the flesh, but of close relatives, or, as exegetes of the old Catholic church maintained, children of Joseph by an earlier marriage. This was fitting for the mother of God. It cannot be reconciled with the worthiness or holiness of the mother of God that after the birth of her divine Son, she should have wished to have other children. In his well known *Dogmatics,* Father Diekamp says also, with a glance at the holy Joseph, that it would not be fitting if he had desired the Virgin Mary after something so great had come to her.

The second privilege that we will name is Mary's immaculate conception, defined as a dogma on December 8, 1854. Many have consistently made the mistake here that this expression means that the Virgin Mary was herself miraculously conceived as was Jesus. It does not mean this. It means that Mary was conceived in a natural way, but

that God from her life's first moment has preserved her
from the contagion of original sin. That is to say that God
in his especial grace has allowed the redemption through
Christ to precede him in her moment of conception in
such a manner that she has never for one moment been
under the curse of original sin.

But together with this, it is the Roman Catholic belief
that Mary is free from all personal sin, even the smallest
of sins. She is entirely and perfectly sinless. That which
no righteous person can escape in life, namely to commit
sin, Mary has been spared by the grace of God. The
Roman church finds this dogma witnessed to in the Bible—
by a correct understanding of the angel's greeting in Luke
1: "Ave, gratia plena," "Hail Thou, full of grace." The one
who is filled with or permeated by grace cannot have sin
within herself. In addition, Roman theologians point to the
passage in Genesis 3:15: "I will put enmity between you
and the woman, and between your seed and her seed; he
shall bruise your head and you shall bruise his heel." Here
the old Latin Bible version is completely unique in its
translation: "*She* shall crush your head," and herein a
prophecy regarding the Virgin Mary was directly read.
If Mary participated in the contamination of original sin,
she could not be the one who would be victorious over the
devil. But even if one translates according to the original
text and lets this prophecy concern Jesus, then, according
to Catholic conception, it is said at the same time that it
also concerns His Mother.

The last privilege is Mary's bodily assumption into
Heaven proclaimed by Pope Pius XII by the bull of Novem-
ber 1, 1950. The dogma is formulated in this manner:
Mary, the immaculate mother of God, forever virgin, after

having completed the span of her earthly life ascended with body and soul into the heavenly glory.

In the bull, the Pope relates how countless requests and prayers had come to the papacy to allow this dogma to become established. Therefore the Pope on May 1, 1946, sent a letter to all bishops with two questions: Are you, reverend brothers, by reason of your great wisdom and knowledge regarding this matter, willing that the most holy Virgin Mary's physical assumption into heaven shall be declared and defined as dogma, and you desire this together with your clergy and all the faithful?

These two questions were answered almost unanimously yes. This dogma cannot claim to have support either in the Bible or in the tradition of the first century. Pope Pius XII is of the opinion in his bull that there is at any rate an indirect support in the Bible and that the various theologians' insights and conclusions in the final analysis rest upon the Holy Scriptures. "This shows us God's Holy Mother bound to her divine Son with the most intimate of bonds, always sharing His fate. . . . As our Savior is the Son of Mary, it was impossible that He who most completely kept the commands of God, should not honor his beloved mother second only to His Divine Father. As He now could honor her with that great distinction of protecting her from the dissolution of the grave, one must believe that He actually has done this."

Except for a legendary reference from the fourth century, we hear nothing about Mary's assumption into heaven until the sixth century when a festival for her assumption was inaugurated. However, it is not completely clear whether this concerns Mary's soul or her body.

At any rate, it is clear that Mary is dead. In and of

herself, she did not need to die since death is the wages of sin and Mary is without sin. Nevertheless, Mary must pass through death because she, as the mother of the Redeemer, must follow her Son in this. Mary's body is not subject to corruption, but immediately after death is reunited with the soul and ascended into heaven. The virginal body from which the God-man had received his own body and blood could not become food for worms as if it were sinful flesh. The glory of the Son forbade this.

2. *Mary's task or mission.* Here also we must first say that Mary is the mother of God. Her most important task was to give birth to Jesus in the world, and to be his earthly mother. But Mary is also the mother of all men, and she is this in a double meaning. In the first place, Mary is the mother of all as she is their refuge and helper in all earthly need. After Mary has ascended to her Son, her work as the church's and man's motherly helper has reached a scope that on the whole cannot be described, says Leo XIII. For now she has reached her pinnacle and heavenly glory, which were due her on the basis of her worthiness and peculiar merits. From eternity it was in the thoughts of God that she should from this day exercise her watchful commission over the church and as a motherly helper stand by the side of man in the battle against all evil. The Virgin Mary knows all earthly needs far more intimately than an earthly mother knows her children's needs. Particularly in the hour of death does she come near to man.

Her help concerns not only the single individual but also whole peoples and, in particular, the church. In answer to the prayer of the Rosary, Mary has often interceded in church history, for instance, against such heretics as the Albigenses in the Middle Ages and the Turks in the sixteenth and seventeenth centuries. Mary's great intercessory prayer halted the terrible second world war according to Pope Pius XII in 1948, and the same Pope in 1942 dedicated all of mankind to Mary and her unspotted heart. "Queen of the Rosary, the helper of Christians, the refuge of the peoples of men, victor in all God's combat, praying we throw ourselves before Thy throne. We are assured that we can obtain mercy and grace and effective help in our present misfortune. We do not presume to expect this because of our worthiness but hope for it alone on the basis of the immeasurable goodness of your motherly heart." Then a prayer of peace for all peoples follows: "We dedicate ourselves to thee and thy immaculate heart, thou our mother and queen of the world, in order that thy love and thy protection can hasten the triumph of God's kingdom and that all people in peace with each other and with God can give thee holy praise, and that they from the one end of the earth to the other together with thee can give voice to the eternal Magnificat of glory, love, and thankfulness to the heart of Jesus in whom they alone can find truth, life, and peace."

Pope Pius XII comes back to this dedication in his great encyclical concerning the church (1943): "We have faithfully dedicated all mankind to her immaculate heart. May she, the mother of all Christ's members, who shines forth in heaven, sanctified in body and soul and ruling together with her Son, obtain from Him without ceasing the richest streams of grace that well forth from the exalted head down to all the mystical body's members! May she also today as formerly take the church under her mighty protection and soon obtain from God more peaceful times both for it and for the whole of mankind."

We have thus already touched upon the second motherhood of Mary—that Mary is also the spiritual mother of all believers. Through bearing the Redeemer in her womb, Mary also bore in a spiritual, mystical manner all those who are embraced by the life of the Redeemer, all those that were to be saved by his work. Therefore all members of Christ's body have likewise come forth from the Virgin Mary's mother life, for which reason all Christians also are called in a mystical manner the children of Mary and she their mother. The most holy Virgin is thus at one time the mother of God and the mother of men, and is blessed by God with an enduring fruitfulness. All who belong to Christ are born of Mary. This is true not only for the believers within the Roman Catholic church, but those who have separated themselves from the one holy church are likewise "born again unto Christ," through Mary. Therefore Mary constantly works for the unity of the church.

With this we have reached Mary's great work as the one through whom all grace streams down to man, Mary as the mediator of all grace. She unceasingly performs that office for God, because she possesses God's whole and complete pleasure on the basis of her worthiness and her merits, and her power supersedes all the holy ones of heaven, even the angelic choirs. God has put all the abundance of good in Mary. Therefore, whatever hope, grace, and salvation is found in us, streams to us from Mary. Such is his will, who now once and for all has decided that we shall have everything through Mary.

For this reason it is said: through Mary to Jesus. As none come to the Father except through the Son, so no one comes to Christ except through his mother: no grace except through Mary. That does not mean that Mary effects grace;

Christ does this, but it does mean that Mary mediates grace
to man. Grace comes to earth and to man as a result of her
intercession. It was Mary, by her mighty intercession, who
achieved the wonderful gifts of the Holy Spirit of Pentecost
that came down to the newborn church. And it is God's
will that everything shall come to us through her. Mary
is, as Bernard of Clairvaux has said it, and as Pius IX repeated it, "the channel" or "the neck that binds the body
with the head." She is "our head's neck through which
all mystical gifts are mediated to His mystical body."

Because Mary surpasses all in holiness and in nearness
to Christ, and is used by him to fulfil his redemptive work
in mediating to us what he has earned, so she is and remains the foremost assistant for the distribution of the
divine grace. It is Christ that sits by the Majesty's right
hand in heaven, but it is Mary who, as the queen of heaven,
stands by his right hand as the proven defender and the
most reliable helper for all who are in danger. The names
of honor that are given to Mary are manifold and the one
surpasses the other, both when they concern themselves
with Mary as a motherly helper in human life or as the
queen of the rosary, of the heavens, even of the universe.
Mary offers not only personal help but also has a salvatory
and cosmological significance.

3. *Mary as a participant in redemption.* We have now
reached a consideration of the final part of her work:
Mary as a participant in redemption. It is true that the
following thoughts about the Virgin Mary have not yet
obtained the official sanction of dogma by the hierarchy
of the church, but it is maintained without question that
the belief in Mary's role in the redemption is a part of the
church's common belief. It is certain that the people of the

Roman Catholic church confidently await that day when this belief and living tradition shall also receive the church's highest acknowledgment and thereby become a truth that is obligatory for all believers. In the many papal circular letters concerning Mary, we time after time find expressions referring to Mary's cooperation in the redemption. It is necessary to understand this expression correctly for it cannot be denied that the word can lead to misunderstanding.

Thomas Aquinas says that there is only one mediator between God and man—Jesus Christ, who gave himself as a ransom for all. But this does not exclude that others in a certain respect can be designated as mediators between God and man insofar as they prepare for and are subordinate co-workers with God for our atonement. Such is the case of the angels and the saints, and the prophets and priests of the old and new covenants. But Roman Catholic theology says that this is true of the Virgin Mary in a completely unique and to a far more extensive degree. There is no one who has contributed as she has, or who on the whole could have contributed so much to God's reconciliation with man. Mary was called to this service from all eternity and as a result is so highly esteemed by her Son and possesses such power that no man nor angel can become her equal. According to the will of God, the redemption of man received its beginning in her. It was her assent to the angel when the birth of Jesus was announced which was the basis for all salvation. In her free assent, which must always arouse our wonder, she agreed voluntarily to become the mother of Jesus and thus gave the Redeemer to humanity which had fallen into eternal corruption. But Roman Catholic theology adds one further thing to this which has far-reaching consequences. It says (and this has been repeated often in the papal encyclicals) that in that moment when Mary gave her voluntary assent, she represented the entire human nature. It was in reality the entire human race which here gave its assent to God's salvation. This corresponds exactly to that view of man which we met in Chapter 4.

But Mary's cooperation in salvation goes wider and deeper, for Mary alone has suffered for us together with her Son. Mary's seven sorrows remind us of this. Of these sorrows, the first three belong to the childhood of Jesus while the last four belong to the suffering and death of Jesus. There is particular reason to mention the last: Mary standing at the foot of the cross of Jesus, *stabat Mater dolorosa!* Here her suffering is fulfilled, for here she unites herself with her Son's suffering for the sake of man. A papal encyclical says concerning this:

"As Jesus was tormented before death in the garden of Gethsemane, as He was beaten and condemned to die, His mother was certainly not with Him, but she knew about all this and knew that it would come. For from the moment that she offered to become the mother of Jesus and in the temple dedicated herself to be a sacrifice together with Him, she received the same lot as He did, namely to atone in the most sorrowful manner for the sins of mankind. Therefore without doubt she felt most excruciatingly her Son's bitter death torment and His painful mistreatment. And it was in her presence and before her eyes that the divine sacrifice was made, for which she in a magnanimous and unselfish manner had nourished the sacrificial lamb at her own breast. At the cross of Jesus stood Mary, His mother. Willingly she gave over her own Son to the divine righteousness, and died herself, spiritually (literally: with her heart, *corde*) pierced by the sword of grief—together with him, in order that she, filled with an overflow of love for us, might conceive and give birth anew."

A later pope, Benedict XV, says the same: "Thus she has suffered together with the suffering and dying Son and almost suffered death together with Him. She renounced her right to motherhood and offered in this manner— insofar as it was up to her (*quantum ad se pertinebat*)— the Son for the reconciliation of the divine righteousness, so that it rightly can be said that she herself together with Christ has redeemed the human race."

"The Virgin of sorrows has together with Christ participated in the work of redemption," said Pius XI, in 1923. There is a difference between the suffering of Jesus and that of Mary. The suffering of Jesus has an infinite value and is in itself (*de condigno*) redeeming. The suffering of Mary has only a limited value and is only substitutionary and atoning by strength of the suffering of Jesus and because Jesus assigns them this value (*de congruo*). By this, Roman Catholic theology intends to have distinguished clearly and sufficiently between the death of Jesus and the death of Mary together with him for the salvation of mankind.

In our day there is a lively debate within Roman theology about what can and should be understood about Mary's part in redemption. There is agreement that the matter belongs to Roman Catholic belief but there is no agreement about how this shall be understood. It may well be that a coming Mary dogma will some day clarify this matter for Roman Catholic Christendom.

Let us conclude this brief presentation by citing one more papal expression, Pius XI's praise of the Virgin Mary in the bull of 1854, in which he proclaimed the dogma of Mary's immaculate conception. The pope first thanks Christ for giving him grace to bring homage and praise to the mother of God through the definition of the dogma of her immaculate conception.

In Mary he puts all his faith and his full trust. "Beautiful and without blemish is she. It was she that stepped on the head of the gruesome serpent with her foot and brought about the salvation of the world. She is the glory of the prophets and the apostles, the honor of the martyrs, the joy and crown of the saints, the surest refuge and faithful helper for all who are in danger upon the entire earth, the mighty mediator and redeemer with her only born Son, the church's most glorious jewel and adornment, and its constant protector. She has evermore nullified all false teachings and delivered believing peoples and nations from the greatest difficulties, even as she has also freed us personally from many threatening dangers."

For a full picture of the Roman Catholic's relationship to the Virgin Mary, it would be necessary to discuss very important things—the worship of Mary and the Mary piety. However, we will have to let this go, and only remark that the preceding discussion makes it clear that the veneration of Mary quite naturally takes a very great place in the Catholic cultus and piety. Mary does not merit adoration which belongs to God alone, and yet she deserves a much higher veneration than that which is shared by the angels and saints, the so-called *douleia*. Mary is honored with a kind of superveneration, *hyperdouleia*. Where the veneration of Mary ceases, there the true church of Christ is no more. To abolish veneration of Mary means to do away with Christendom and thus overthrow God's plan.

For where Christ is, there is also Mary. And only where Mary is, is there Christ.

There is probably no place where the difference between the two understandings of Christianity becomes so plain as in their differing conceptions of the Virgin Mary. Evangelical theology knows that this teaching point of Romanism has often been distorted, and knows that it has a duty to clarify the Roman insights on this point as authentically and as reliably as possible. But as Evangelical theology gains insight into the Roman view of this question, and sees how completely penetrating the role of Mariology is and how intimately it is knit into the deepest motives in Roman Catholicism, it grows in understanding how different the Evangelical and the Roman Catholic traditions are. And especially in times where what we have in common becomes more evident and stronger, what is divisive bursts forth suddenly and painfully.

First, we will give the Evangelical criticism of this Roman Catholic teaching, and then give an account of how Evangelical Christendom looks upon the Virgin Mary, the mother of our Lord, in a positive way. For here, in the middle of that "no" which divides, is also a matter which we have in common, and which it is important to underline.

1. *The Evangelical Lutheran view of the Roman Catholic Mariology.* Both churches will maintain the apostolicity of the church. According to the Evangelical Lutheran view this means agreement with the biblical apostolic witness to Christ. To the question of whether the Roman Mariology is contained in and agrees with the witness of the apostles, Evangelical theology must answer "no." It sees in this teaching the consequences of not recognizing the Scriptures

as the only source of revelation. Evangelical theology does
not see every dogmatic development in tradition as a
change of, or an addition to, the biblical apostolic witness.
One need only recall Luther's view of the creeds of the
primitive church. But when the Evangelical theology confronts Roman Catholic Mariology it must judge this development of the post-apostolic faith as contrary to its
biblical basis. Here, more than any other place, it becomes
clear what can happen when the stream of tradition is
made into the criterion of truth; when the differing streams
of religious beliefs with their notoriously different sources
are made into sources of faith and revelation. Mariology
shows Evangelical theology that not scripture and tradition,
but tradition alone can be a source of revelation in the
Roman church.

In opposition to this, the Evangelical church must again
assert its view of scripture as the only source of faith. The
Evangelical church cannot recognize that Mary dogmas
by virtue of a papal definition can be made into the truth
necessary for salvation. The apostolic church never knew
Mary in the way that the Roman church today teaches
about her, and venerates her. The apostolic church's confession of Christ thereby becomes poorer and less perfect
than the confession of the Roman church! When the
apostolic witness, as given us in the early confessions and
writings, does not have room for Mariology as this is taught
today in the Roman church, then Evangelical Christendom
must cling to the biblical witness against the development
of Roman teachings.

Without wishing to belittle the often deep religious
motives that lie hidden in Mariology, Evangelical Christendom must ask what has led to the worship of Mary.

Can one not find in Mariology the development of a natural primitive religious need which has its roots elsewhere than in God's clear word and revelation? Is not the dogma of Mary's physical assumption into heaven derived from legend and elevated into a doctrine necessary for salvation? And has the church thereby not become more the Lord over the beliefs of her children than fellow worker for their joy? Or has the Roman Catholic church not actually exercised altogether too little authority by not saying a decisive and definite "no"? These things the Evangelical church must think and ask when it considers what has brought about the Roman Catholic Mariology.

It is not easy for the Evangelical church to say that the Roman church has here abandoned the apostolic basis. The Evangelical church can only do this if it will itself become conscious anew of the apostolic witness to Christ, and also engage in energetic combat against a theology that would volatilize the message about Christ into a gnostic redeemer-myth, so that it now becomes necessary to extricate the creed from a so-called demythologizing. Evangelicals must to an equally high degree refute those who without apostolic authorization seek to add new truths of faith that would be difficult to defend against the charge of mythologizing the Christian gospel. Many Christians throughout the world have felt this Mariology as a heavy burden that weighs not only on the Roman Catholic church but upon their own churches as well.

We come now to a further consideration. Evangelical theology sees in the Roman Catholic Mariology a hindrance to faith in Christ alone. It recognizes that the Roman theology will deny this and yet it must take this stand. It must say its "no" to the constantly growing parallelism

between Christ and Mary. There are given the same titles
to Mary as are given to Christ, even if these are subordinate under Christ. According to the witness of scripture, Christ is the only Savior and Mediator, who
distributes his salvation and grace through his Holy Spirit
in his word and his sacraments. He alone is the one who
has become man, and before him stands the *entire* human
race, including the Virgin Mary. No one other than Christ
himself dispenses grace and salvation.

Although Roman theology maintains that Mary is and
remains a creature, nevertheless, she has been elevated
through her privileges so high above the rest of the creation that it is not easy for the Catholic people and for the
rest of Christendom to escape the conclusion that a creature
has here been made into a divinity. She stands now on the
side of God and Christ opposite that of mankind. It is
through her that all grace is mediated. The phrase,
"through Mary to Christ," obscures that way which God
through his revelation in Christ has shown his church and
in which he advises it to go.

In studying Roman Mariology, an Evangelical Christian
often receives the strange impression that the role which
belongs to the Holy Spirit in the mediation of salvation has
been assigned to Mary. Roman theology naturally does not
intend this, but its view of Mary as the queen of heaven
who distributes all grace to us from her place at the side
of her Son, and who is the way to Christ for us, corresponds
at any rate in some manner to the belief in God's Spirit, in
whom alone there is a way between us and God. A self-
sufficient Mariology, according to the Evangelical view,
disturbs the fact that faith is bound to God alone.

Roman theology's conception of Mary as a representative

for all of human nature is also foreign to the Evangelical mode of thinking. This bold proclamation of Mary's co-operation in salvation, in which she assents to and thereby works together with God on behalf of all humanity, limits God's free grace and sovereignty in salvation. Evangelical Christianity also knows that salvation does not occur "independently" of man, but its belief in salvation as God's work alone is a strategic point to be guarded. Therefore it cannot go along with the interpretation of Mary's "Let it happen to me according to Thy word," for which Roman Catholic theology derives its wide-reaching implications of Mary as representative of all human nature, which in this moment gives its assent to God's purpose of salvation. The teaching about Mary thus becomes a teaching about human nature. This is consistent enough when one considers the entire Roman view of salvation; but the Evangelical view must seriously ask the Roman as well as its own church if a serious fault in the basic viewpoint itself does not lie here. Karl Barth says in his dogmatics that Mariology is a sickly formation in theological thought. And as such it must be cut away.

Finally, Evangelical Lutheran theology must ask if the Roman view of Mary can actually be reconciled with that view of the mother of Jesus which shines forth throughout the New Testament account. The Roman church will maintain that the least of all there is to say about Mary is found in the New Testament. The Italian historian, Ricciotti, is supposed to have said that Mary's biography could be written on only a few pages. Even if others will perhaps find this exaggerated, it is correct that the historical figure of Mary as we find it in the New Testament is less important. Mary has vital importance as a "theological" figure. Here first begins her "format." "It is not as a Biblical figure that she is a problem; but as God's co-worker and as mother of the Son of God and thereby in relationship to saved humanity and to the reborn universe," says Peter Schindler, a Danish Roman Catholic theologian. "It is not the historical figure of Mary that concerns us, but the theological Mary: Mary's role in the drama of salvation from God's eternal plans to the final restoration of all things."

We shall not attempt to discuss here the biblical account of Mary. It does occur to Evangelical Christians that Roman Catholic Mariology often places a meaning in single references that these words could not possibly carry. They read later beliefs concerning Mary into these passages, which very easily distort these references to Mary because they are set into a context which is foreign to the biblical account. As a main result it is forgotten that the biblical picture does not place the mother of our Lord on the side of God and Christ, but together with the rest of mankind. Significant here are these violent words which Jesus in a very critical moment speaks to his mother and his brothers or relatives. "And looking around on those who sat about him he said, 'Here are my mother and my brothers! Whoever does the will of God is my brother and sister and mother'" (Mark 3:34-35). Or the word from Luke 11:28 where Jesus answers that woman who bursts out in wonder over the one who is the mother to him, "Blessed rather are those who hear the word of God and keep it." The last that we hear about Mary is that she, with the apostles, participates in the common prayer, after the ascension (Acts 1:14). After that she disappears completely out of the Evangelical account as quietly and as humbly as she stepped into it. There is here no sign of her "theological format."

2. *The positive side of the Evangelical view of the Virgin Mary* confronts us with no small problem. The "no" of the Evangelical church to Roman Mariology has largely excluded a positive view of Mary. The more the worship of Mary grew in the Roman church, the more indifferent Evangelical Christianity became in respect to her person. The overwhelming "positive" development on the one side was met by a proportionately "negative" attitude on the other. This was not beneficial to Protestant theology or life, as it disclosed weaknesses and needs that were a consequence of something in the basic character of Protestantism. Here also were buds of deviation from the apostolic witness to Christ, buds that did not constitute minor undergrowth but grew tall and strong.

This was not in accord with the stand of the Reformers, for in them, not least of all in Luther, we meet a positive view of the Virgin Mary and an understanding of the fact that Mary truly has her place in God's plan of salvation. Her person shall therefore not simply be considered as that of an unimportant individual, but must be placed within the context of the great biblical, theological, and historical account of salvation. The difference between the Roman Catholic and the Evangelical Lutheran view exists not only in the mere difference between a "yes" and a "no," but also in the widely different opinion of the significance of Mary, a difference reflecting the difference which recurs on all other points. These following concluding lines can only be considered as a broad sketch of the Evangelical understanding of the person of Mary.

In the Roman consideration, the biblical account is only the seed from which the whole plant develops. For the

Evangelical viewpoint, the biblical account is the most important, in fact, the only foundation. The Reformers did not hesitate to call Mary the mother of God. For them, the expression from the Council of Ephesus, *Theotokos*—the one who gave birth to God—is not an unbiblical addition, but fits exactly with the biblical witness. Luther constantly calls Mary the mother of God in his sermons, a term in and of itself strange and shocking, containing the whole secret of the incarnation: true God and true man. God's Son has an earthly mother. It is interesting to note that Luther sees in the Christian confession of the miraculous conception of Jesus in the womb of Mary not only a witness to our Lord's divinity but also to his full humanity. Here he is in full agreement with the oldest theology of the church. He explains the second article of faith in this manner, "I believe that Jesus Christ, true God, born of the Father in eternity, and true man, born of the Virgin Mary, is my Lord."

Mary is the earthly person whom God chose to give birth to and to bring up Jesus. Through her he received his humanity. through her he became fully and completely human. His humanity was not a shell or a deception, but he was "in truth" man. This happened through Mary. Luther expressed it in this manner: "He became that which I am" (*fit quod ego sum*). This ought to be underlined in contrast to an understanding of Christianity which sees Jesus only as a prophet or model. Christ is not only a voice, nor is he only an ideal. Christ is truly the Son of God, born of a woman unto the world.

It is not important to explain here how Christ could at the same time be God and man—that belongs in another important context. But it is important to hold securely to the basic fact of the incarnation: that Christ truly comes wholly out of God and wholly out of man. Therefore it is really of fundamental significance to confess that he was born of the Virgin *Mary*. This point underlines a truth of salvation that Protestant theology has been about to give up in its attempt to make the person of Christ more an idea than a real, living, historical figure which just like this *man* was wholly and fully of God. Mary's significance, underlined by our naming of her name every time we confess our Christian faith, exists first and foremost in holding us firmly to the significance of the person of Jesus Christ.

The biblical account also tells us something about Mary, the chosen one, the mother of the Lord. In his beautiful explanation of Mary's song of praise, *The Magnificat*, Luther considers in some detail the greeting of the angel found in Luke 1:28. The Vulgate, Latin translation of the Bible, has the well-known expression *"Ave, gratia plena."* "Hail Thou, full of grace." The Greek basic text has an expression that means, "Hail, you who are favored of God." that is: you, to whom God in this moment gives great evidence of grace. The Greek verb *charitein* is used only one other place in the New Testament, in Ephesians 1:6, as an expression for forgiveness. "Full of grace" would make necessary another Greek expression *"plaeraes charitos,"* an expression which is used twice in the New Testament, about Christ as the only begotten Son of God (John 1:14) and about Stephen, an early Christian (Acts 6:8).

The expression "Hail, you who are favored of God," does not express something about Mary herself but about God's marvelous and gracious action toward her. There is found nothing in the expression about Mary's nature in and of itself, but it recognizes that God bends down to her and shows her a grace that shall be shared by the whole human race, through her. She is chosen by God to be that person through whom the miracle of incarnation shall take place.

"For he has regarded the low estate of his handmaiden" (Luke 1:48). The Latin translation here has the word *humilitatem,* which leads one to think of humility. Luther maintains strongly that it is not a quality of Mary that God takes notice of, but her low estate and littleness, her *Nichtigkeit* that the Greek word means. That which is nothing in the eyes of the world, the unnoticed, that without esteem—this is exactly what God chooses when he wants to carry out his salvation.

For this very reason all generations shall praise her as holy. Luther maintains that Mary does not claim much good will be said about her or her virtue will be praised— neither her virginity nor her humility nor her sinlessness. Nothing will be sung for her own achievement, but mankind will praise her solely because God has done this deed to her. Because God saw her in her low estate and chose her, the generations will say of her that she is holy. Not she, but God's great deed toward her and thereby toward the entire human race, is to be praised.

One notices an obvious difference in the whole tone of this from the Roman Catholic Mariology. What is determining is Mary's significance here on earth, not as the queen of heaven. She is the great witness here on earth of how God acts when he saves, by choosing that which in the eyes of the world is nothing; even more: by leading those he chooses out into the darkness and temptations of faith. The Roman understanding of Mary stands as an expression of a "theology of glory," the Evangelical as an expression of a "theology of the cross."

In *Fear and Trembling,* Kierkegaard emphatically maintains that Mary's entering the need, the torment, and the paradox is what made her great. "To be sure, Mary bore the child miraculously, but it came to pass with her after the manner of women, and that season is one of dread, distress, and paradox. To be sure, the angel was a ministering spirit, but it was not a servile spirit which obliged her by saying to the other young maidens of Israel, 'Despise not Mary. What befalls her is the extraordinary.' But the Angel came only to Mary, and no one could understand her. After all, what woman was so mortified as Mary? And is it not true in this instance that also that one whom God blesses He curses in the same breath? This is the spirit's interpretation of Mary, and she is not (as it shocks me to say, but shocks me still more to think that they have thoughtlessly and coquettishly interpreted her thus)—she is not a fine lady who sits in state and plays with an infant god. Nevertheless, when she says, 'Behold the handmaid of the Lord'—then she is great, and I think it will not be found difficult to explain why she became the mother of God. She has no need of worldly admiration, any more than Abraham has need of tears, for she was not a heroine, and he was not a hero, but both of them became greater than such, not at all because they were exempted from distress and torment and paradox, but they became great through these." [1]

I have included this entire selection because it says something essential about the Evangelical view of Mary. One hears talk of the "Protestant Madonna": that poor woman holding the child upon her lap so cozily and mov-

[1] Walter Lowrie (trans.), Søren Kierkegaard's *Fear and Trembling* (Princeton University Press, 1941), p. 99.

ingly. There exists no "Protestant Madonna"—but in the Bible there is painted, or perhaps rather suggested, a picture of a woman who was chosen to be the mother of the Lord and must therefore enter into great pain and agony, into the darkness of faith where there was no outward sign of the miraculous word that she had heard, but where she must fight against temptation and doubt. She must offer that which stands closest to a mother's heart, her child, and here she renounces all privilege and precedence before others, and as a completely ordinary person together with all others must live on His word and grace alone. Even if she were His mother, the chosen and favored one, she should not in any respect become an exception.

In a crucial moment, she did not understand her own Son, but doubted his call. The Bible tells us that she stood by His cross, but it does not tell us that she in that moment was clear about what was happening there, offering her divine Son to God and thus being with Him in the redemption. Maybe she understood nothing; maybe she also belonged to those that saw Him die in shame and disgrace and there had to see the hope of her life disappear. The scriptures say nothing of this. We only hear that after the resurrection she was with the apostles, the brothers of Jesus, some women, and prayed. In no respect is she distinguished from the others. With this information the New Testament account of her comes to an end. She is at one time the chosen mother of the Lord and at the same time a completely ordinary member of the first little circle about the Risen One. The Evangelical view sees something very great in this; perhaps in this there even lies something greater than in the whole Roman Catholic viewpoint: Mary completely taken up in the service of the life of the Son of God here upon earth, a service she fulfils in faith and obedience if not without temptation and struggle.

In the liturgy to a feast of Mary it is said, "In the entire world you alone have brought all heresies to an end." If we correctly understand the New Testament words about Mary, it can perhaps be said that Mary in her position in biblical history protects us by her humility and by her faith, against the temptation of worshiping something human. She who received the greatest task that ever has been assigned to any woman to fulfil—to be the mother of Jesus—plays an entirely self-effacing role in the biblical account until it allows her to disappear into obscurity. She is the great witness to Christ himself, who alone is that word of God in whom we as well as she shall place our hope.

In this manner the New Testament allows Mary to stand in the story of salvation as one completely unique and favored—and as an ordinary person in faith and hope. This is what we hear and therein lies something exceptionally great. Therefore Mary's name shall not disappear in anonymity but shall be recalled in every age and praised as holy. Evangelical Christendom must also learn to sing this song. For both in the choice to be the mother of the Lord and through this to be the instrument for that event which alone is the life and the hope of the world; and in that faith which God gave to her in which she said, "See, I am the handmaiden of the Lord. Let it happen to me after Thy word," as well as in the "dread, distress, and paradox," as Kierkegaard expressed it, she points to Christ as the only Lord and Savior—for herself as well as for all mankind.

The Roman Catholic view is clearly formulated to the minutest theological detail and constantly awaits further papal definitions of dogma. The Evangelical view is barely suggested, extremely modest, and yet is powerful for those who are sensitive to it. The dividing line between them is clear and decisive. The difference does not need to be stressed further. Hardly anywhere does the mutual "no" and the alienation between the Roman Catholic and the Evangelical stand out so clearly. It is as if all the lines from all else discussed in this book run together here.

And yet this cannot make the two parties abandon one another. Even in the midst of what most profoundly separates them, they are gripped by a "yes" which is larger than themselves and which neither of them is able to change over to a "no." And this "yes" is not based on greater or lesser agreement upon many or few points, but alone on the crucified and risen Lord himself. If the weight is laid only upon the viewpoints and opinions of the "schools," or even upon the catechism to which the two churches feel bound, then the "no" is the dominant and actually the only possibility. But if the sight is directed in faith to the living Lord as he appears in the witness of scripture and in the creed of the church, then the most energetically outspoken mutual "no," from whatever side it comes, is put in its place by one greater, Christ himself. In him alone is a common "yes" securely anchored.

Type used in this book
Body, 10 on 13 Caledonia
Display, Caledonia bold
Paper: White Standard G. M. Antique